Praise for *How Can I Be Your Lover When I'm Too Busy Being Your Mother?*

—

"Nothing he does is good enough for her, and she's not affectionate the way she used to be. If this sounds familiar, help is here in the form of an in-depth guidebook called *How Can I Be Your Lover When I'm Too Busy Being Your Mother? The Answer to Becoming Partners Again.*"

—*Maclean's*

"*How Can I Be Your Lover When I'm Too Busy Being Your Mother?* tracks how the 'mother syndrome' is laying waste to marriages. . . . The authors call on both genders to defy obsolete societal values, urging men to step up and women to step off."

—*The Globe and Mail*

Praise for *Character Is t[...]*

—

"Sara Dimerman makes a convincing case that developing character in our children is one of a parent's most important tasks. In *Character Is the Key*, she provides an innovative, step-by-step template for families who want to explore the values they cherish and deepen their commitment to living by those values."

—**Caroline Connell**, former editor in chief, *Today's Parent* magazine

"Dimerman provides strategies for unlocking the best in our children— and in ourselves—and then gets specific with techniques for acquiring the attributes of empathy, fairness, courage, honesty, initiative, integrity, optimism, perseverance, respect, and responsibility. *Character Is the Key* gives parents hope and the tools they need to raise kids with good character and bright futures."

—**Susan M. Heim**, author of *Susan Heim on Parenting* blog

Praise for *Am I a Normal Parent?*

"Like therapy for the mind and soul. . . . The whole concept of what 'normal' is, is so beautifully contemplated in this book. . . . Thank you for this invaluable insight."

—**Kim Galway** from Richmond Hill, Ontario

"As a mother who reads a lot of parenting books, I found *Am I a Normal Parent?* to be incredibly helpful. . . . Sara gives concrete advice and suggestions that truly helped me with my three kids. . . . I found out that I *am* a normal parent!"

—**Karen Horsman**, broadcaster

"Should be deeply comforting to anyone who has ever suffered the guilt and anxiety that is woven into the parenting experience. Sara Dimerman makes it clear that you're not alone as she shares the honest input of hundreds of parents, along with her own hard-won nuggets of wisdom."

—**Adele Faber**, co-author of *How to Talk So Kids Will Listen & Listen So Kids Will Talk*

WHY
married
couples
DON'T HAVE
SEX

(. . . AT LEAST NOT WITH EACH OTHER!)

SARA DIMERMAN

Published By Simon & Schuster Canada

New York London Toronto Sydney New Delhi

Simon & Schuster Canada
A Division of Simon & Schuster, Inc.
166 King Street East, Suite 300
Toronto, Ontario M5A 1J3

Most of the stories, vignettes, and anecdotes in this publication were
made up by the author to illustrate points. Some are loose composites
of experiences shared with the author. A few are adapted from real life.
Identities have been changed.

This publication contains the opinions and ideas of its author, and is
intended to provide helpful and informative material on the subjects it
addresses. It does not render personal health or other professional advice
or services to readers, who should consult their own qualified health
professional before adopting any of the suggestions in this publication or
drawing inferences from it.

The author and publisher specifically disclaim any responsibility for any
liability, loss, or risk which is incurred in relation to the use or application
of any of the contents of this publication.

This Simon & Schuster Canada edition February 2015

SIMON & SCHUSTER CANADA and colophon are registered trademarks
of Simon & Schuster, Inc.

For information about special discounts for bulk purchases,
please contact Simon & Schuster Special Sales at 1-800-268-3216
or CustomerService@simonandschuster.ca.

Manufactured in the United States of America

1   3   5   7   9   10   8   6   4   2

ISBN 978-1-4767-6770-3
ISBN 978-1-4767-6771-0 (ebook)

This book is dedicated to my husband, Joey, as thanks for his love and support over more than thirty years

〜

Contents

~

How This Book Came to Be

T HE IDEA FOR this book came to me as I sat in a circle of women on the floor of a dance studio at a Salsa Moms and Babies group. I had been invited to talk about "life after baby" to a dozen moms with babies under a year of age. I planned to talk about the changes they might be experiencing within themselves and in their relationships with their partners. As I waited for their exercise class to end, I watched the moms mimic their instructor as they grooved and gyrated to Psy's "Sexy Lady." Their babes were steadfastly held in Snuglies and attached to their waists—some asleep, heads bouncing, others staring wide-eyed into the large mirror in front of them. After the class ended, I sat with these women on the floor of the dance studio and led a discussion.

The dance instructor broke the ice by sharing how she was convinced that the stretch marks she had developed on her stomach during pregnancy were the reason her husband no longer seemed to find her as attractive and how she covered them up by always wearing a nightshirt when they were having sex. Another mom shared how she wasn't going to have sex with her husband until she could fit back into her pre-pregnancy jeans. Over the course of an hour, the moms became increasingly comfortable with sharing. All of the stories had similar and familiar themes, and as each woman shared her own tale, others were more inclined to do the same. Towards the end of the session, one mom concluded that basically everything we'd talked about led back to a single topic: changes to their relationship in the bedroom. "It all leads back to sex," she said. "Sometimes I want to just tell him to go get it somewhere else because the reality is that I'm just not into it."

I have been counselling couples for almost twenty-five years, and the number one complaint I hear from married men is that they're not having enough sex (with their wives). So I can't say that I was surprised to hear what these women were telling me. But the workshop, combined with my counselling experiences, got me thinking about what's going on in the bedrooms of married couples. Clearly there's a problem—at least for some. I decided to look into the issue more deeply.

Do women really want less sex? To hear men tell it, this is certainly the case. And plenty of women seem to back this up. Often I've heard a woman complain about how her husband is constantly horny; she may even confess that she purposely goes to bed early so that she can pretend to be asleep by the time he shows up. Or she may find herself in the company of a group of friends who, after a couple of glasses of wine, commiserate about their sex lives, laughing out loud at the stories they share in common—which typically involve husbands who are portrayed as never being able to get enough.

But does all of this anecdotal evidence really suggest that women don't want sex as often as men, or is there more going on beneath the surface? Maybe the answer is a bit of both. On the one hand, research does suggest that even in "good" relationships, women tend to desire sex less often than men. In 2005, the Global Study of Sexual Attitudes and Behaviors (GSSAB) surveyed 13,882 women and 13,618 men, aged 40 to 80 years, from 29 countries. The goal was to study various aspects of sexual problems and relationships on a global level. One of the study's findings was that 26 percent to 43 percent of women experienced low sexual desire, compared to 13 percent to 28 percent of men.[1] This certainly seems to confirm what I have heard at social gatherings as well as in my practice.

On the other hand, however, it may be possible that women have different standards. It's my experience that women are more likely than men to complain about not having "good" sex, and that "bad" or "unsatisfying" sex is often one of the reasons we give for not wanting to be intimate with our partners. (It's interesting to note that many of my female clients, initially petrified about being alone and getting naked with another man following divorce or separation, report later that they never knew sex could feel so good.) Is it possible that men are better equipped to enjoy sex than women? After all, it's hard for a penis not to feel good in a warm, tight environment. If a man can attain and maintain an erection, it's easy for him to have his sexual needs realized. Why wouldn't he want to experience this as often as possible? A woman, on the other hand, doesn't always feel good with a penis in her vagina. The penis has to be angled just right, has to rub against other parts in just the right way in order to heighten stimulation, and there has to be enough lubrication. In addition, she may be less able than her male partner to put aside any emotional baggage she might be carrying around in order to enjoy the experience fully. In other words, it's perhaps not so simple for a woman to have "good" or "satisfying" sex. And it stands to reason that if you are engaging in unsatisfactory sexual experiences, you will not want to engage in those experiences as often. Even if sex is not so bad, if you go without it for a long time, you miss it less and less. Like potato chips: the more you have, the more you want, but if you refuse that first chip, you will likely be okay with not having any.

Further complicating things for women on the intimacy front is the fact that there's been a marked change in the way women handle dissatisfaction in a marriage. There was a period in time when wives were expected to do their wifely duties and that was that. If you weren't happy with how things were playing out in the bedroom, you didn't talk about it with your friends, or even—for the most part—with a therapist. You put up with it and carried on. Nowadays, though, women are no longer afraid to assert themselves when they feel that their physical and emotional needs are not being met, and even to retreat from sex that is not satisfying. So, while it's possible that many wives are not interested in sex with their husbands, this doesn't necessarily mean that they are asexual. Instead, a woman may choose to rely on personal pleasure such as masturbation, or be equally as likely as her mate to look elsewhere to satisfy her sexual needs.

The good news, of course, is that sexual intimacy—like many other issues within a marriage—is something that can be explored, understood, and improved. Once a woman has figured out what turns her on (and off), found ways to communicate this to her partner, and seen the beginnings of changes in their sexual relationship, she too may desire sexual intimacy as much and as often as (or more than!) her husband.

And that, in a nutshell, is why I decided to write this book. Wherever I happen to be, the mere mention of its title is enough to reinforce my belief that most married couples can relate to some aspect of this topic. After hearing the first part of the title—

Why Married Couples Don't Have Sex—men and women both take playful jabs at one another with responses such as, "Well, we could definitely use that book on our bedside table, couldn't we, dear?" *Nudge, nudge. Wink, wink.*

The most affirming response I've received to date came when I was chatting with the wife of a couple who owns a coffee shop I frequent. She asked one day how I was doing, and I mentioned that I was feeling a little overwhelmed at the idea of having to submit a manuscript to my publisher by the end of the month. "Oh," she said, "what's the book about?" As soon as I mentioned the part about married couples not having sex, she excitedly ran to the open door of the kitchen, where her husband was baking muffins. "Honey," she exclaimed, "a lady at my counter is writing a book for us!" When she returned with my coffee, she wanted to know how and when she could get a copy—the sooner the better, she said. Inevitably, people want to know more. Most of us love to talk about sex and are curious about other people's sex lives. Maybe it's the voyeur in all of us. Maybe it's because we can then compare our sex lives to theirs. Maybe it's so we can live vicariously through their experiences, because we're afraid to try them ourselves. Or maybe we want to learn more than we already know.

Over the course of this book, I will explore patterns and dynamics that occur between couples and the problems that may be creating boulders on the path towards healthy sexual intimacy and fulfillment. Whether or not you're on the same page about how or when the problem began and how to fix it, it is vital that you be able to talk about where you're at as individuals and as a couple, and about how you can meet each other's needs at the same time as identifying and taking care of your own. On the pages that follow, I'll show you how to do just that—and how to bring intimacy and sex back into your relationship.

Introduction

The State of the Union

IF YOU ARE reading this book, chances are you have questions or concerns about your sexual relationship with a significant other. You may be worried that you're not having enough sex, or perhaps that you're wanting too much. You may be concerned about the fact that you no longer seem to desire sex the way you once did, or that your spouse doesn't seem to desire you. You may be running out of excuses to put off a partner with a much bigger appetite for sex, wondering why you find yourself constantly relying on excuses, and questioning why there's such a disconnect between the two of you.

Perhaps you simply miss having sex, remembering that it made you feel more connected to one another. Perhaps you've convinced yourself that you're okay with just cuddling and hand-holding, because deep down you don't believe that either one of you is willing or able to make sex more exciting. Or perhaps you're having a hard time getting beyond the negative emotions that are dividing you. Perhaps you have given up or lost hope.

Does any of this sound familiar? If so, rest assured that you aren't the first person to worry about intimacy within a marriage—

and you won't be the last. How you and your spouse relate to each other in the bedroom is a key factor in the health of your relationship, and the fact that you are ready to explore some of the issues around this topic is a terrific sign that you are ready to take steps towards improvement. In the pages that follow, we'll look at some of the common problems that crop up around sex within marriage. We'll explore the excuses that women (and, to a lesser extent, men) offer for a diminished sex drive. And then we'll dig a little deeper to get at the truth behind the excuses. I'll also suggest some exercises that can help bring intimacy and sex back to a marriage. These exercises are critical to re-establishing the connection you and your spouse once shared. Time and again I have found that couples who are active communicators—those who talk to each other about feelings, thoughts, and needs both in bed and at other times—are more likely to maintain an emotional connection. This, in turn, leads to increased intimacy and a desire to spend time with one another. Ultimately, this increased intimacy leads to an improved sex life, even when you least expect it. And the bonus? Better sex leads to more sex. Better sex plus more sex equals a more happily married husband *and* wife.

Before we start down this path, though, let's sort out some of the basics.

Defining Sex and Marriage

Since part of the title of this book is *Why Married Couples Don't Have Sex*, let me start by defining what I mean by *sex* and *married*. For the purposes of this book, the word *sex* refers to vaginal or anal intercourse. Although I recognize that sex may include any sexual act or behaviour between two or more consenting adults, I have purposely separated intercourse from other sexual behaviours or intimacy. In my experience, when men complain about not having enough sex, or women complain about not being in the mood, they are typically referring not to foreplay or other displays of intimacy but to intercourse itself. This is not to say that I won't be addressing other ways in which couples can enrich their sexual relationships and intimacy, just that I am separating these from the act of intercourse.

When I use the word *married*, I mean not just those of you who have officially tied the knot, but any couple who lives together. Even though I use the pronouns *he* and *she* and pair penises with vaginas, I am aware that same-sex couples also experience issues in the bedroom and may benefit from reading this book.

Defining Normal

Now that we've tackled the definitions of *sex* and *married*, at least as far as this book is concerned, let's turn our attention to another word that's regularly thrown about when discussing sexual relations within a marriage: *normal*. Unfortunately, trying to define what's normal in terms of sex is just about as difficult as trying to define what's normal, or typical, in any other part of life.

Not surprisingly, one of the things you find when you delve into the topic of how often couples are typically having sex is that other factors are significant, most specifically age and the passage of time. Over the years of working with couples, I have noticed that dating couples tend to rank highest, with many having sex practically every time they see each other. Couples who are very newly living together or wed (with no kids) typically have sex approximately two to three times a week. A year later and you're looking at about once a week, and after kids the number likely drops to less than weekly.

If you're looking for more "scientific" data, you may be interested in a Kinsey Institute[1] research paper that concluded that 18- to 29-year-olds have sex an average of 112 times a year, 30- to 39-year-olds an average of 86 times a year, and 40- to 49-year-olds an average of 69 times a year.[2]

Some of these numbers are consistent with the findings of Dr. Harry Fisch, a New York–based urologist, internationally renowned sexual health expert, and author of *Size Matters*, who has conducted research on the frequency of sex for married couples at different ages. His results reveal that for married couples under the age of thirty, the frequency (on average) is about twice a week. However, this drops to about once a week for couples in their fifties.[3]

For some couples, statistics like this are reassuring. For others, however, they can be cause for concern.

The Sexless Marriage

What if you're a married couple who isn't having sex once every week or two (when the stats indicate you'd be "normal" if you were)? What if you and your spouse are having intercourse less often? My experience has indicated that even these seemingly low numbers might be higher than "normal" for the average married couple with kids (or post-kids). Perhaps my stats are skewed because I'm working with couples who are already experiencing difficulties in their relationship, but I'm inclined to think not. Evidence suggests that I may be right.

A 2009 *New York Times* article bearing the headline "When

Sex Leaves the Marriage," states that "about 15 percent of married couples have not had sex with their spouse in the last six months to one year."[4] These findings were consistent with a *Newsweek* report that "15 to 20 percent of couples have sex no more than 10 times a year."[5] But 15 to 20 percent of couples is in fact a low estimate when compared to the results published in a book, *7 Keys to Lifelong Sexual Vitality: The Hippocrates Institute Guide to Sex, Health and Happiness.* Authors Brian and Anna Maria Clement report that 30 percent of American men and 28 percent of American women said that they were either celibate or had sex only a few times a year.[6]

To put this in perspective, what the stats above reveal is that if you're out for the evening with two other couples, chances are that at least one couple is living in a sexless marriage; if you're sitting with five friends, it's likely that at least two of you are having sex less than ten times a year. And keep in mind that respondents to sex surveys may tend to overestimate their sexual activities so as to feel better about their situation. If this is the case, it's quite possible that well over 30 percent of married couples are having very little sex indeed. So, if you're concerned about the decline of sex and sexual desire in your marriage, and if you're feeling angry, sad, or disappointed, then you're not alone.

Who Says You're Not Alone?

Well, I do. But I too am not alone in this belief. Many well-researched and respected studies have shown how typical these changes are and how curious people are about whether their relationship is different from or the same as others' relationships.

Of all the reasons couples seek counselling with me, problems in their sexual relationship ranks high on the list. They often want me to get in the middle of their debate over what constitutes a "normal" amount of sex. When I am asked for my opinion, I may share some of what I've read and seen, but I also make sure to mention that what's good for one couple might not be good for all. And I tell them straight from the start that my role is not to judge how much is too little, just enough, or too much. Finally, I tell them that I am much less concerned about the number of times they are having sex each week than I am about how content each partner is with his or her sexual intimacy (quantity without quality will likely not lead to sexual satisfaction); the underlying individual reasons that each has for wanting more or less than the other; and the impact that their sex life is having on their relationship in general.

If either one of you—or, in the best-case scenario, both of you—believes that sex is highly important for relationship satisfaction and therefore feels quite dissatisfied, and if you're willing to work at getting desire and satisfying sex back, then you're already on the right track. As with the couples who come to see me in my practice, my goal is to help you work towards the realization that the state of your sex life is a reflection of deeper issues in your relationship. Once you begin to understand why you (and possibly your partner too) are feeling and behaving in a way that inhibits your sex life, you can share the real reasons you do not wish to be intimate with one another and start working at making things better.

Part of this book will address the *At Least Not with Each Other!* part of the title. When you're talking about sex within marriage, it's impossible not to bump up against the issue of infidelity. After reading this book, you will have a much better idea of how and why husbands and wives choose to engage in sexual or intimate relationships with others. It is my hope that you will then be able to make educated, informed decisions before embarking down this road yourself (if you haven't already!).

Whatever your reasons for wanting to read this book, I'm sure you will not be disappointed. The key to bringing sex, sexual desire, and intimacy back to life is figuring out what has led to the current state of your union, and then deciding what you're going to do about it. Are you ready? I'm sure you are. So let's get started.

Part I

What's the Problem?

One

Sex Isn't the Issue

F YOU'VE GOTTEN this far, two things are clear: first, you are not entirely thrilled with the state of things in your bedroom; second, you are willing to work at making a change. This is a great place to start. The important first step, then, is to figure out what's at the root of the issue. Why isn't your sex life as satisfying, adventurous, and pleasing as it once was, or could be?

The clichéd answer—and the one you will likely hear the most when casually exploring the subject—is "lack of desire." Sometimes, that lack of desire is even attributed solely to women. ("Women just aren't as interested in sex as men," you'll hear people say.) That answer may be common, but I'm not at all convinced that it's true. As mentioned in the introduction, I believe that women of all ages would very much like to be having more sex, and more sexually fulfilling relationships. We're certainly surrounded by sex these days—in the media and as consumers—and women seem to be enjoying it just as much as men, if not more so.

The *Fifty Shades* Phenomenon

If I'm looking for evidence to back me up, I don't have to go much further than my local bookstore, where I'll find the shelves stocked with *Fifty Shades of Grey*, *Fifty Shades Darker*, and *Fifty Shades Freed*, by E. L. James. The erotic trilogy has sold more than 100 million copies worldwide and has spawned a host of copycat series all determined to tap into this previously underserved market.[1]

Fifty Shades of Grey may not have been in the running for a Booker Prize, but its success is certainly a testament to the fact that women want to be seduced and desired, to be whisked away from their boring sex lives, and to explore hot new ways to bring passion and pleasure back into their lives.[2]

What I've come to think of as the *"Fifty Shades* phenomenon" is not, in fact, an isolated case. Perhaps spurred on by the book itself, or, more likely, by the open dialogue about sex and intimacy that it's encouraged, women are beginning to look beyond the bookshelf in their quest for a more fulfilling sex life.

Beyond *Fifty Shades*: Sexy Consumer Shows

Couples are now flocking to expos such as the Everything to Do with Sex Show. This show—the first of its kind in Canada—is held annually in several cities and is a "three-day consumer adult event geared towards anyone looking to spice up their life," says show manager and co-owner Mikey Singer. Adults can attend seminars and visit exhibitor booths for the latest and greatest in high-end sex toys and erotica or watch a sexy stage show together. "As more people have become more comfortable with their sexuality and women have gotten more involved in the business and made more demands on the people making the products, their quality has improved," says Singer.

Singer thinks it's great to be part of an organization that he believes is doing good. "When we can help a relationship come together instead of breaking up, that's a good thing," he says. "In fact, the standard line at our office is that we're saving relationships, one sex life at a time."

As a testament to the fact that women are now more heavily involved in figuring out what works for them in the bedroom, the 2013 Halifax show's stats reveal that more than half of the attendees were women. In Toronto, 65 percent of attendees were married or in a relationship.

Since the event began, in 2000, the number of people attending in Toronto, for example, has grown fivefold (from ten thousand in 2000 to more than fifty thousand in 2013), indicating not only a desire among adults to spice up their sex lives, but an openness and willingness to seek out and learn new ways to embrace and enhance their sexual relationships.

When both partners recognize the impact of a poor sex life on their relationship in general, they seem to be more inclined to seek out ways to spice things up. Attendees at the Everything to Do with Sex Show, for example, flock to the ever-popular educational programs. Ranging in age from mid-twenties to mid-eighties, attendees pack the room of seminars such as Steamy Hot Oral Sex and G Spot, P Spot (P referring to a man's prostate). "The Pleasures of Anal Sex seminar is always filled to the back," says Singer, apparently unaware of the pun. "I'm going to be thirty-five this year, but when I was twenty-seven I would see my parents' friends in there."

Liz Lewis Woosey, president and show manager of Black Kat

Shows, and producer of the Sexapalooza consumer show, shares numbers that support what Singer has seen in terms of attendance. The attendance at the Toronto Sexapalooza show has grown from eight thousand in 2010 to twelve thousand in 2013. Liz runs her consumer sex shows all year long in several cities across Canada and in Columbus, Ohio.

She believes that their show, like other consumer sex shows (Taboo, the "naughty but nice sex show," runs similar expos in Canada's western provinces), is attended by those who want to be entertained and educated and who love to shop. The demographics tend to be similar across all of these kinds of shows, she says, noting that Sexapalooza has recently initiated a "sexy senior" discount ticket for the many over sixty-five who attend.

Sex Shops: Still Going Strong

When I was growing up, a naughty must-see for any tourist visiting Toronto was Yorkville's Lovecraft. After being raised in South Africa, where censorship (and other forms of conservatism) was rampant and magazines such as *Playboy*, which hit the stands in 1953, were banned, I was especially fascinated! In the bright, well-lit store (no dingy "head shop" atmosphere here), one could find everything from vibrators to edible underwear. Although the shop has now moved to the suburbs outside of Toronto, Lovecraft, until very recently, was owned and operated by Anne Amitay, one of the original two women who established it almost four decades ago, and it's still working hard to ensure that couples have satisfying and adventurous sex. A quick peek at the store's website, for example, reveals FAQs such as "What do ben wa balls do?"; "Is a vibrator the same as a dildo?"; and "Do you have 'couple friendly' DVDs?"

Like Anne Amitay, Carlyle Jansen, founder of Toronto's Good for Her shop and an expert on modern-day sexuality, has also long known the importance of educating couples about how to inject flavour into their relationship. Along with other trained facilitators, Carlyle has offered workshops for individuals and couples since 1997. Since opening its doors, Good for Her has grown by leaps and bounds. They sometimes offer workshops every night of the week—mostly out of their location in downtown Toronto, but also at consumer shows or even with groups of people, sometimes in private homes.

"Sex" outlets and boutiques like Lovecraft and Good for Her aren't unique. Shops like these can be found in cities around the world. Some, like Chicago's G Boutique, are for women only, while others, such as Ann Summers (UK) and Beate Uhse (Germany), are open to everyone. There's also a growing online presence including bestvibes.ca and PinkCherry.ca (or Pink Cherry.com).

* CARLYLE'S COME A LONG WAY *

Carlyle Jansen says that when she was younger, she was "not comfortable with sex. I avoided it through my teen years, wasn't comfortable having sex until my early twenties and then found that I couldn't orgasm—neither on my own nor with a partner." She decided that she needed to learn more about sex, began watching videos and reading books, and soon discovered the Hitachi magic wand, which did the trick: she was able to orgasm—finally!

And at her sister's (a United Church minister) bridal shower, Carlyle realized how much information she had acquired about sex. She became the expert after giving sex toys to her sister as her gift and then responding to all of her friends' curious questions about them. Afterwards, people commented about how comfortable she seemed talking about sex and how she should offer workshops. She did exactly that through the YMCA, but after women talked about wanting a permanent safe and comfortable place to go to, Toronto's Good for Her was born in 1997.

A Museum of Sex?

There's a Museum of Bad Art in Boston, and a Museum of Parasites in Tokyo, so is it any wonder that there's a Museum of Sex? Daniel Gluck, native New Yorker and founder of the Museum of Sex in Manhattan, believes that sex is a subject that people are more comfortable with than ever before and that it's become more normal to talk openly about it.

Since its opening, in 2002, when they saw around 70,000 people (50 percent tourists and 50 percent locals) come through the door, the museum's numbers have grown tremendously. As of 2014, they see about 190,000 visitors annually, ranging in age from those in their twenties to seniors coming in with walkers. Around 65 percent of those visitors are female.

Gluck believes that people come to the museum for three things: curiosity, titillation, and education. Sexuality, he says, is a subject to which most, if not all people, have a personal connection.

The museum's growth is yet another reflection of what people are talking and wanting to know more about—sex. Gluck says that "people have lusts and desires and there are a variety of ways to enjoy them. It's becoming more normal for people to discuss and explore their sexual desires and pleasures in a much more honest and open way."

Sex on Screen

Television shows and movies with a high and more explicit sexual content are nothing new. Visit a movie theatre or turn on a television or a computer and you'll likely be able to find a host of sex-related content (never mind steamy sex scenes that are included as a matter of course). There are also a host of sex advice shows that viewers can tune in to at any time, thanks to PVRs and "on-demand" viewing. But recently, I came across something that seems to perfectly underline our growing interest in learning how to improve our sex lives. Courtesy of a YouTube link that my fifteen-year-old sent my way (she had seen mention of it on her favourite radio station's Facebook page), I learned about *Sexbox*. In this UK television show, three sex therapists and a moderator converse with couples right after they've had sex in a concealed box on the stage. The concept behind the show is unique: the producers reason that because a couple is at their most vulnerable and open to talking about their experience right after having sex, that's when it's best to ask them questions. While they're in the box, the experts chat with the host about different topics related to sex, such as how the Internet has changed the face of pornography and how important it is for kids to be critical viewers of porn so as to mitigate its damages. Once the box's light has gone from red to amber, the couple emerges to answer questions such as "Do you feel closer?"; "Was that a good experience for you?"; "Did you talk much?"; "Did you let your partner know what feels good and what doesn't"; and "What do you define as good sex?" Shows such as these—though unconventional and controversial—certainly make for interesting and often informative watching and also continue to create open forums and opportunities for people to discuss sex.

—

So, clearly, sex is all around us. It's in the pages of the books we're reading, and on our television, movie and computer screens. It's become a tourist attraction and a consumer-show market. It's even a booming business. Just ask Noel Biderman, founder of Ashley Madison, the popular online dating service for married men and women, whose site now has over twenty-six million members around the globe and growing.

Faced with our obvious interest to know more about sex, can we really say that a lack of desire is at the root of our problem? Should we really believe that women, in particular, don't want to have sex, and don't want to explore new and creative ways to do so? I think not. But that answer begs another question—one that begins to get a little closer to the real reasons why so many married couples are dissatisfied in the bedroom: If lack of desire isn't the problem, then what is?

Two

Is It All in Our Heads?

OR MANY OF us, sex is about much more than what goes on between the sheets. In fact, how we feel about sex—from our desire to have it through to how satisfying or disappointing it is when we do—is affected by what goes on between our ears. Sex may be a physical act, driven in large part by physical urges, but it's also an emotional demonstration of our feelings. And so it should come as no surprise that how we think and feel really does have an effect on our sex lives.

Women, in particular, appear to be prone to having their dial dimmed or turned right off by things going on around them. Imagine you're in the middle of making out with your spouse when he burps in your mouth. Ugh! What a turn-off! He didn't mean to, but that hardly matters—you push him away in disgust and any arousal you were experiencing is completely gone. Or let's say you're in the middle of having sex when your teenager turns the lock in the front door. Even though your bedroom door is shut and he knows not to come in without knocking first, your arousal suddenly crashes from an eight out of ten to a zero. Your husband doesn't seem affected—in fact, he amps up the speed at which he's thrusting in and out of you, eagerly anticipating his orgasm—but you want him out of you now that your teenager is home.

Are men prone to the same turn-offs, or are their sexual responses driven primarily by physical needs? We've all heard jokes about men thinking with their "little head" rather than the one on their shoulders. And it's true that a man's penis will sometimes get him into trouble, or at least give him away (it's hard to hide the evidence of a man's sexual arousal, involuntary or otherwise). So, what's a guy to do? Once his penis is erect and ready for action, he can either help return it to its flaccid state by engaging in some action (either on his own or with a partner), take a cold shower, or send some very loud and clear messages from his "big head" so as to let it down gently. This last option may not sound appealing, but it is possible.

I was reminded about the power of the mind when a client Ryan (you'll read more about him in chapter 7 and "Ryan," as with any names of clients I refer to, is a pseudonym) shared that he and his spouse, who had not had sex for several months, often showered together. I asked what happened when he got an erection in the shower; he said that he didn't get one. After I expressed surprise, he shared that since he did not want to create conflict between them about having sex, he purposely did not "allow" his penis to become erect in the shower, even though he still found his wife physically attractive and could have had an erection if he opened his mind to it. This was a reminder to me of how powerfully the brain manages all aspects of our body's functions, including our sexual response.

Along with helping you better understand how messages are carried between the brain—the command centre of your body—

and your sexual organs, I'm also going to be answering the following questions: Are women truly more vulnerable to dramatic dips in arousal? What inhibits sexual desire and arousal in both men and women, and what causes sexual dysfunction? Are the discrepancies between men and women's levels of mental and physiological sexual arousal due to differences in their brains, their anatomy, differences when aging, or simply differences in the way they think? In other words, how much of the difference between men and women when it comes to sex is attributable to neuropsychology versus physiology?

Brain Basics

Let's begin by examining the brain in plain English, the limbic system in particular. The limbic system regulates things like emotions, memory, sexual arousal, and desire, and it works in very close partnership with the nucleus accumbens, the brain's pleasure centre, which plays a role in sexual arousal. However, arousal is highly dependent on the amount of dopamine projected from the limbic system.

Activities such as sex increase dopamine levels, and dopamine turns on your reward circuitry. You can think of dopamine as the "Gotta have it!" neurochemical, whatever "it" may be (sex, alcohol, a certain food or drug). It's the "craving" signal: the more dopamine you release and the more your reward circuit is activated, the more you want or crave something.

For both males and females, the natural production of dopamine is at its highest during orgasms, especially following intercourse. In fact, brains that are experiencing the "Big O" resemble those experiencing a heroin rush.[1] This is why, after great sex, you feel like you could go a second or even third round. But there's a flip side to that coin. If you stop having sex for weeks or months, the craving cue is switched off, and you are less likely to desire it.

Dopamine is the motivator, but endorphins—which are produced in the hypothalamus (part of the limbic system) and the pituitary gland (which is neurally and chemically connected to the hypothalamus) and released during sex—allow us to enjoy the experience. You may have heard exercise junkies talk about how the release of endorphins during a workout makes them feel good and keeps them coming back for more. Apparently, people who engage in certain behaviours—such as watching porn, drinking a large amount of alcohol or going to casinos on a regular basis—may become addicted to these activities because their dopamine levels are also being boosted each time they engage in them.[2]

So, if you are finding that your desire for sexual activity with your partner has really declined and you can't figure out why, you may want to ask your doctor to check your dopamine levels. A dopamine deficiency often leads to lowered libido, among other things (interestingly, an excessive amount of dopamine can lead to sexual addiction and fetishes).[3]

Oxytocin is another hormone that factors into our feelings about sex and sexual intimacy. It too is produced in the hypothalamus and released by the pituitary gland in both partners during sex. Unlike dopamine and endorphins, however, the release of oxytocin plays a role in the creation of an emotional bond (oxytocin is also released during childbirth; the more oxytocin a mother releases, the smoother her labour).

* THE PIONEERS OF SEXOLOGY *

We owe much of what we know about how the human body responds to sexual activity to some renowned pioneers of sexology, including Dr. Alfred Kinsey. Regarded as the first major figure in American sexology, Kinsey began as a zoologist at Indiana University. He courted controversy in his career and personal life: he was bisexual and lived in an open marriage. He founded the Kinsey Institute at Indiana University in 1947.

Walking the same controversial path were two other well-known pioneers in the field: Dr. William Masters, a gynecologist, and Virginia Johnson, initially hired as his research assistant (they married in 1971). Together, they became world-renowned as sex researchers, teachers, and therapists.

Despite challenges and opposition, Masters and Johnson found men and women (including themselves) who were willing to quite literally expose themselves. In their "lab," the pair observed, monitored, and recorded information about the human body's physiological response to arousal and sexual activity before, during, and after intercourse and masturbation. They confirmed that unlike the very obvious changes that a male body experiences during sexual arousal, the changes to a woman's body need to be examined much more closely (which they did, with the aid of a specially rigged camera!). Much of what is happening physiologically when a woman is aroused is not obvious to the naked eye. For example, during the four stages of arousal—excitement, plateau, orgasm, and resolution—non-visible changes occur in a woman's body. These include clitoral swelling, changes to the vaginal lips and entrance, and contractions of the vaginal and uterine muscles if she orgasms.

In 1964, Masters and Johnson established their own independent non-profit research institution in St. Louis, Missouri, called the Reproductive Biology Research Foundation. The centre was renamed the Masters and Johnson Institute in 1978. They worked together for almost forty years, but the relationship ended after they divorced in 1993. Though their institute closed in 1994, their legacy lives on.

Messages from Home

Having some idea of what makes us tick on a physiological level is important, but it's equally important to know that what goes on in your head is not only related to hormones and neurotransmitters. Depending on the family in which you were raised, messages from your parents and others close to you—both taught and passively passed down—will have influenced your views on sex. If you grew up in a home where sex was never discussed, or intimacy was never shown, you may find yourself feeling uncomfortable discussing or engaged in it. If, on the other hand, you were raised in a home where sex was regarded as a natural and comfortable part of life—perhaps your parents showered together, or scheduled "alone time" when you were asked not to interrupt them—

you may thank them now that you are grown, because home is where you likely first learned that sexual intimacy is something special, not shameful. (And, by the way, it's normal if the thought of your parents having sex with one another once made you shudder—as your children now do at the thought of you having sex!)

Let's take a quick look at some of the shameful, negative messages about sex and sexuality that have an impact on the current state of your relationship.

Sex Is Wrong

On their website, Betty Dodson and Carlin Ross, well-known and respected sex educators, write that "sexual repression begins with the prohibition of childhood masturbation."[4]

If you grew up believing that sex was dirty; that masturbation led to warts and blindness(or, in Indonesia, decapitation)[5]; and that only sluts allowed boys to touch their breasts, let alone their vaginas, before marriage, then these thoughts are now engrained in your brain, like them or not.

Sex Is Dirty

Maybe no one came right out and told you that sex was wrong, but you may have gotten that message anyway. If you weren't allowed to eat with your fingers because sticky hands were a no-no, or if you were quickly ushered into the house after playing in the muck outside so that you could scrub your hands, you may have grown up feeling less comfortable with bodily fluids too. As an adult, you may rush to wash your body (or your sheets) after intercourse instead of relaxing in your lover's arms. No wonder you feel that sex is too much of a chore!

Sex Is Taboo?

Reflect back on how your parents talked about their bodies and yours. Were penises and vaginas referred to by their proper anatomical names, or were cute or silly "code words" used instead? If you grew up in a home where the vagina and penis were just as comfortably spoken about as any other body part, where menstruation and wet dreams and pubic hair were not taboo, then you are likely to be more comfortable speaking about your sexual needs and what turns you on and off, and learning about what to do to heighten your desire and arousal.

You'll Get Pregnant!

This may be a message that we more typically associate with parents and their adolescent daughters, but even married adults share this concern. Unless the female partner is on birth control pills, and therefore pretty much certain of not conceiving, is post-menopause, or has had a hysterectomy, or unless the male partner has had a vasectomy (and even that is not 100 percent fail-safe), some couples may avoid sex because they are worried that even with a condom, his sperm will somehow find their way to her eggs.

Some couples may fear becoming pregnant before they are ready or after they already have their desired number of children. Some women even have such an intense fear of pregnancy or childbirth that this phobia has been given a name: tokophobia. But regardless of how extreme her worry is, sexual desire—for her or both—will be inhibited as a result.

A Double Whammy

Clearly we're all carrying around messages—some special and positive, some shameful and negative—from our younger years. That's sometimes hard enough to deal with, but what happens when your brain and your body combine forces to really throw things off-kilter, when something physical triggers a reaction that sends your brain into a tailspin? This double whammy happens more often than you'd think, and both genders are susceptible.

Performance Anxiety

If fear of pregnancy is often thought to be a primarily female concern, sexual performance anxiety is associated more with men. Men, especially those who have had even one negative experience before or during sex, may disengage from their spouses for fear of the same happening again. Wives often take this personally, assuming that they are no longer attractive or sexually appealing to their husbands. This may be far from the truth, but it may be difficult for a man to talk about his performance anxiety with his wife. He may fear that she will see him as less manly or capable, or he may simply feel awkward broaching the subject, especially if they typically don't discuss their sex lives with one another.

A survey of urologists and sexual medicine experts from sixty countries estimated that about 40 percent of adult women and 30 percent of adult men suffer from at least one major sexual dysfunction.[6] Dr. Laurie Betito, a Montreal-based psychologist, author of *The Sex Bible for People Over Fifty*, and host of a nightly radio show called *Passion*, says that she has heard and seen a change with regard to performance anxiety issues for men over the past twenty years. Years ago, she says, "the typical guy with erectile dysfunction was in his sixties. Now he's much younger." She attributes this change to unrealistic expectations men may have for themselves and their partners, mostly as a result of what they see in the media, including in pornographic images.

Many men (or their wives) contact clinics for help, while others take matters into their own hands (thinking that the problem may be that they are less interested or less turned on by their wives) and look outside the marriage for another woman who will "fix" the problem. Carol Bresgi, founder and managing director of Canadian Men's Clinic, says that "sometimes—especially if the erectile dysfunction is mild—he is successful with someone new, but not necessarily because the problem is with his partner but because he is much more sexually aroused in a different and new sexually provocative environment." She says that she would never recommend this to anyone as a way of overcoming performance anxiety.

Seeking professional help (for assessment and treatment) is certainly better than trying to figure things out on one's own, as a proper evaluation will often reveal that the problem is physical as opposed to psychological or related to sexual chemistry between the couple. For the majority of patients who are reassured that their problem is more than likely caused by physical changes (arterial sclerosis, venous leakage and, less typically, nerve damage, can all, according to Bresgi, be causes of erectile dysfunction) there is relief that the problem is not, as many initially assume, just in their "heads."

✳ CANADIAN MEN'S CLINIC ✳

Carol Bresgi founded Canadian Men's Clinic in Toronto in 1997 to help couples experiencing difficulties in their sexual relationship as a result of male-related concerns such as erectile dysfunction (the inability to obtain or maintain an erection), premature ejaculation (a male psychosexual disorder in which ejaculation occurs soon after sex begins), and low sex drive.

Bresgi says that for men, premature ejaculation is especially embarrassing. For some men—the majority aged forty and older—Canadian Men's Clinic is not their first stop in seeking help. They may have already seen their family doctor, but even after treatment haven't noticed any or much change. Many are given pills as the first line of treatment, but unfortunately these have side effects and don't work for everyone, she says. As a result, men become even further discouraged, thinking that their problem is so extreme that even their doctors and "the miracle pill" can't help. So, they come to the clinic feeling desperate, with high hopes that they will find a solution to their problem. She lets them know that treatment works differently for everyone, that doses may need to be tweaked or other treatment options explored over a period of time. This is why Bresgi calls the work that they do at the clinic "more of an art than a science."

Hormone Woes

Women too can experience reduced desire as a result of physiological changes—and the results can be just as confusing and frustrating for them as they are for men.

∗ GINA ∗

After her first marriage ended, Gina had a string of relationships with younger men. They made her feel younger and more attractive and things were definitely hot in bed. Gina's libido was comparable to the men she knew: she was horny and wasn't afraid to let men know it.

When I met Gina, she was involved in a more serious relationship with a man her age. They had been living together for just over two years. Although she still found her boyfriend attractive, she realized that they weren't interested in having sex as often. She worried that she would never feel the same sex drive again. She also knew that a permanently rotten sex life would be a deal breaker for her.

Gina asked her partner if he had noticed a change in their sex life. He said he had, but that he hadn't expected that it would always be as good as it was at the beginning. He reassured her that she was just as attractive to him as ever, and that he was content to have sex less frequently—especially since he felt that they maintained strong intimacy through cuddling, foot massages, and hot hello and goodbye kisses when either left or came back from work.

Not completely satisfied with this, and worried that she had lost her mojo, Gina consulted with a medical doctor who offers alternative medicine options. After a consultation and testing, Gina learned (with relief!) that she was deficient in testosterone. She was diagnosed with female sexual arousal disorder and prescribed a customized cream that she could rub on parts of her body as directed. Within a couple of weeks, she noticed an increased desire for sex, and she was more responsive when her partner touched her.

Gina is not alone in her experience. In 1999, Edward Laumann—a sociologist and leading authority on the sociology of sexuality—and associates, conducted a study in part "to assess the prevalence and risk of experiencing sexual dysfunction across various social groups" in the US. They reported that 43 percent of women experienced some type of sexual dysfunction (the most common complaint was low sexual desire), compared to 31 percent of men.[7]

Dr. Rebecca Bodok, a family physician and founder of the Toronto-area Vital Transitions Clinic, has seen and treated numerous cases like Gina's. She says that there are many reasons for low libido at different ages and stages in a woman's life. As with Gina, however, low testosterone appears to be the culprit for many women, and it can occur as early as in their twenties. Some women are actually born with a lower level of testosterone but aren't aware of it until they become sexually active, she says. Even though a woman's level is always less than a man's, problems can arise when it drops below what is normal for females.

Men who are experiencing low libido (sometimes in combination with fatigue) should also have their testosterone levels checked. Unlike women, men don't experience the complex up-and-down hormonal cycle that women do on a monthly basis. Their hormones typically remain pretty constant throughout their post-pubescent lives, only declining naturally as they age.

Some men experience symptoms associated with erectile dysfunction as a result of this decline, yet others don't see or feel any difference.

As women age and enter menopause, Dr. Bodok says that the primary symptom leading to low libido is vaginal dryness. This often causes a vicious cycle: vaginal dryness leads to painful sex, which leads to anxiety about having sex, which causes women to back away from or avoid sex. Sometimes a vaginal estrogen cream can prevent this cycle and allow women to enjoy sexual experiences more.

Other than a hormonal imbalance, decline, or deficiency, there are several other physical and environmental conditions (or complications as a result thereof) that can cause low sex drive or unsatisfying sex. These include thyroid problems and diabetes, for example, low iron levels (anemia), sleep deprivation leading to fatigue, stress, mental health issues, side effects from taking certain prescription drugs, and even excessive biking![8]

As you can see, a comprehensive assessment of all possible physical, psychological, and external causes—including determining whether there may be a history of sexual abuse, for example—is a must when exploring why a couple is not having much or any sex.

Everyday Concerns

Along with life experiences, physical concerns, and pesky hormones, troubling thoughts or worries (about sex and other things) can negatively affect your ability to relax your mind, and therefore your body.

Think about the times when these nagging thoughts affected intimate moments with your partner. Some of the questions below may jog your memory. For example, do you:

- Always have one ear open to make sure that the kids are still asleep or occupied?
- Have a difficult time disconnecting from what still has be done for tomorrow's meeting at work?
- Worry about how you're going to pay the bills by the end of the week?
- Think about the hurtful comment he made about your parents earlier on in the day?
- Wonder whether he was really out with his best friend the night before?

Did you put a mental checkmark next to any of the above? If so, it's likely that your body will follow your mind's distracted lead. Instead of enjoying the intimate experience, your performance may be robotic and detached. If your spouse picks up on your detachment, he might ask where your head is. Likely thinking that it's not the right time to talk about an earlier argument or your financial worries, or wanting to avoid conflict, you might apologize and come up with something like "I'm just really tired" or "I'm not feeling that well."

And without even giving it all that much thought, you would have found yourself slipping into the most common pattern I find in couples who are experiencing problems with intimacy and sex: making excuses.

Three

Excuses, Excuses

W E ALL KNOW the word *excuse*, but what exactly does it mean? According to one of the definitions of the verb form, offered by dictionary.com, *excuse* means "to release from an obligation or duty." And, yes, for many women, sex is just that—an obligation and/or a duty. Some might even call it a burden. So, don't think you're alone if you believe that the best part of having sex with your partner is when it's over and you can breathe a sigh of relief knowing that you have a reprieve from having to perform for at least a few nights, maybe even a week or two. (One woman, upset at her husband for compiling a spreadsheet that documented the number of times she had refused sex, along with a list of her excuses, actually posted it on social media for all to see, looking for guidance and support from other wives!)[1]

For many of us, excuses are often presented in the form of justifications. These justifications—tried and true after centuries of use— are designed to be hard to ignore, or at least to lead to a bit of guilt.

Which of these common excuses have you used to get out of having sex?

1. "I'm too tired."

2. "I'm not in the mood."

3. "I've got a headache."

4. "I've got to get up early in the morning."

5. "I'm preoccupied with work."

6. "I'm angry with you."

7. "I can hear one of the children."

8. "You need a shower."

9. "I've got a bad back."

10. "It's too soon in our relationship."

Sound familiar? They should! The list above is taken from a "top ten" ranking of excuses that people use to avoid having sex, according to a 2009 survey conducted in London, England. The results were revealed after conducting research with four thousand British adults. The researchers also shared that "one in five Brits regularly make excuses to avoid having sex" and that "seven out of ten said they were often too exhausted to enjoy sex."[2]

In a 2013 babble.com article entitled "Twenty Excuses Women and Men Use to Get Out of Having Sex" (although the majority seem to have been shared by women), writer Devan McGuinness offers old familiars, along with some that are not as common:

"I think I forgot to take my birth control."

"I just made the bed."

"My horoscope advised against it."

"The dog is staring at me" (With two cats and a dog on our bed at night, I can relate to this one!)

"I cut myself shaving and it is a no-go-zone."

"I ate too much dairy and now I'm bloated."[3]

Anatomy of an Excuse

Whether you're relying on a tried-and-true favourite (like the classic headache excuse) or something more creative (your horoscope), an excuse is still an excuse. Or is it? Surely it's possible that you might actually have a headache or a bad back? Let's look at some of these excuses a little more closely before we move on.

✳ SEX AS HEADACHE CURE? ✳

Those of you who use the slightest pain in the head to get out of having sex might not want to let your spouse know that, according to a team of German neurologists, sex was actually found to cure or diminish the symptoms associated with a migraine or cluster headache in more than half of the sufferers they surveyed.[4] About half of the questionnaire respondents noticed an improvement in their headaches following sex (this was particularly true for male sufferers). However, upon closer inspection, it's clear that it's not actually sex, per se, that improves headaches but the resulting orgasm, which doesn't always occur and can also—sometimes even more easily—be achieved through masturbation.

Too Tired

Top on the hit parade of excuses for not having sex is being too tired. It's almost ironclad. After all, how can one argue against someone's being tired, especially when most of us are run off our feet every day? However, some may argue that sex or sexual play can be rejuvenating or improve stamina. Let's explore this in greater detail. It makes sense that when you are stimulated—through massage, for example—your body may come alive. Add to this the intoxicating sensual smell from a musky oil, and—voilà!—you may feel turned on as your senses come to life. The problem is that after you've been married for a while and had a couple of kids, you're usually not thinking of romance and ways to arouse one another's senses. You're more likely just looking to have sex and get it out of the way so that you can have a better night's sleep or cross sex off your to-do list that week.

The bottom line is that for many, setting the mood and putting effort into waking your partner's senses just seems like too much work, especially when you're already tired. Sometimes, it's just simpler to turn your back to your partner and pretend to be somewhere between half asleep and dead to the world as you mumble, "I'm sorry, I'm just too tired."

Use this excuse at night after a long harried day and it might fly. Use it in the morning after a restful sleep and you may have a little more convincing to do. In fact, you may need to come up with another more plausible reason for not wanting to have sex. Better yet, it may be time to examine the real reasons you're not excited about having sex with your partner and figure out whether you'd prefer to explore ways to have a more sexually fulfilling relationship.

Not in the Mood

Second on the published list of the top ten excuses is "I'm not in the mood." The problem with waiting until you're in the mood for sex is the same as waiting until you can afford to have children. If you wait until you're horny enough to have sex or until you have enough money stockpiled away to have kids, you may never have sex or become parents—outcomes that may, in fact, be related to one another!

What exactly does not being in the mood mean? Our mood is our emotional state of mind. For many of us, mood is related to our environment—what's going on around us. But mood can also be related to our general disposition, worries, or stressors at any given time. So, when we say that we are not in the mood to go out, we may mean that we don't feel that we can muster up the energy to leave the house, or that we'd rather not be in the company of others. However, if your spouse suggests that he will take the kids to the park so that you can have a nap, he may find you more "in the mood" for going out later. Similarly, even though you may not be in the mood for an intimate exchange with your spouse after you've had an argument with your mother, for example, things may change after a while, especially if your partner has made an effort to take care of you, rather than relying on you to take care of him or others.

Not Feeling Well

You can take "I've got a headache" and "I've got a bad back" and lump them together under a catch-all "I'm not feeling well" excuse—another pretty common one, when you search it out in all its guises. As with the "too tired" classic, it's hard to argue against. How can your partner refute the fact that you are not feeling well? He might ask whether the feeling is physical or emotional and might ask what he can do to help, but again, if he has any heart, he will not force himself on you when you are not feeling well—

whether feigned or not. The problem with the excuse of not feeling well is that it can lead to a self-fulfilling prophecy. You may begin to actually feel unwell as a way of adding legitimacy to your claim. The other fallout from this excuse is that your spouse may begin to see you as not being very well and may, as a result, feel about or behave differently towards you. The bottom line is that, if used when you are likely not feeling as unwell as you're saying, this excuse may take you down a road you hadn't anticipated.

The Kids!

Kids can indeed put a crimp in a couple's sex life. They make you tired, they sometimes stress you out, and when new moms are breastfeeding, they may feel less inclined to want physical contact with their partners. As the kids get older, you may truly be concerned about a child's walking in on you (maybe even to save *them* from being traumatized!), especially if you haven't had a "privacy please" sign hanging over your doorknob since they were very little.

And when they're a little older still, most nights you will often legitimately be ready for sleep earlier than they are. Trying to be discreet when you're having sex or even just making out in bed is quite difficult and, for women in particular, is not conducive to their feeling relaxed enough to enjoy the experience.

Real or Not?

So, are excuses real or not? Do they have an ounce of truth hidden somewhere inside, or are they pure fiction, designed to help you avoid doing something you really don't want to do?

The answer is likely "all of the above." Not feeling 100 percent can be a convenient excuse to avoid sex if you really don't want to have it. If you did, chances are you'd get by! Feeling tired can be a good reason for saying no, but imagine if your partner climbed into bed with you and very slowly and tenderly touched you in ways that turn you on. On some occasions, you might just be willing—and happily so—to let yourself be woken up in that way.

The key with excuses, then, is to understand how, why and when you are using them. Are they used only on occasions when you're really not in the mood? Or are you pulling them out of your hat on a regular basis? Do you ever work ahead of time to legitimize your excuse? Maybe you begin to role-play early in the day so that you appear more convincing at night. Or perhaps you invite one of the kids to have a "sleepover" in Mommy and Daddy's bed that night.

If this—or something like it—describes the state of things in your marriage and bedroom, chances are that your spouse may start to get suspicious. An excuse, used once or twice, and offered at infrequent intervals, is rarely given a second thought. However, if excuses—legitimate or not—are made every time your spouse reaches for you (or most of the time), then this is cause for concern. After a while, your partner will likely doubt that you are truly tired every time he wants to have sex. He may get a sense that you are avoiding being intimate with him. Or he may get worried and suggest that you see your doctor.

If "I'm not feeling well" has become a perpetual excuse, then wouldn't it make sense for you to try to find the cause and cure for your headaches so that you can enjoy a more satisfying sexual relationship? Despite being urged to get help for your chronic complaint, you may find yourself resistant to your partner or a therapist's suggestions. Sometimes your push-back is a way of saying "Leave me alone. I'm an adult. I know what to do." More commonly, though, your lack of motivation is either because you're not feeling as bad as you say (and therefore don't see the need to consult with a professional), or because the excuse is serving a purpose and you'd rather have the real headache than deal with the headache of having sex.

In my experience counselling men, I've learned that they're not as unfeeling or thickheaded as women sometimes think. They have feelings too, and these feelings are hurt by repeated excuses. They feel unwanted, undesirable, and rejected. In time, they too may start to make excuses or begin behaving in a passive-aggressive manner so as to give you a taste of your own medicine— sometimes consciously, sometimes not. Instead of offering a verbal excuse or initiating a conversation about how hurt he feels, he may start rejecting you—sometimes in the subtlest of ways. Perhaps he'll stay up later than you and avoid joining you in bed. Or maybe he'll bring electronics to bed and wait for you to fall asleep before he disconnects from his iPad. Maybe he'll actually fall asleep while you're in the bathroom flossing your teeth and taking off your makeup.

If you've noticed this change in your partner's behaviour, you may want to consider the message behind *his* actions as well as your own. Perhaps you're only too happy for him to be acting this way—it gets you off the hook and allows you to appreciate the luxury of a bed all to yourself—but is this really the relationship you had envisioned? A relationship you would wish on your children? A relationship in which you have to look for excuses— most of which are conjured up or exaggerated—so as to create or maintain distance between you? A relationship in which you'd both rather turn your backs to each other than put your feelings into words? My guess is that this isn't what you envisioned and hoped for, and that's why you're reading this book. If I'm right, then pat yourself on the back—you've taken an important first step. Excuses are built and maintained on underlying emotions, and these will not change until each excuse is identified, examined, and resolved. Through this process, those old excuses will fall by the wayside, allowing each partner to expose their vulnerability so that they can stand in pure nakedness, with increased vitality and a desire to connect with one another in the most intimate act of all—sex.

Why Not Tell the Truth?

So, if all these excuses aren't helpful or good for your relationship, and if you know, on some level, that you have to address the underlying issues, why not just tell your spouse the truth? My bet is that you'd say that it's not worth the trouble it might lead to. Maybe you've tried being honest in the past and found that it led to lots of arguing at a time when you'd rather be sleeping. Let's break this down. Say, for example, you're still mulling over a mean comment your spouse directed towards you earlier in the day. He's apparently unaware of how it affected you, or he's totally forgotten about it by the time he slides over to your side of the bed and moves his body close to yours. When you continue to lie there, not moving an inch, he enquires as to why you're giving him the cold shoulder.

In this moment you have a choice: you can either make up an excuse, such as being tired or having a headache, or you can tell him the truth. The truth might sound something like: "You were mean to me earlier on today so I'm not interested in being intimate with you right now." In the ideal world, he would want to discuss this some more, after which he would take responsibility for his behaviour, explore ways to respond differently next time, apologize, and ask for your forgiveness. In fact, all of this pillow talk might be quite a turn-on for you and might actually lead to your wanting to be intimate with him after all. However, in the real world, he is more likely to get defensive, feel rejected, and accuse you of finding reasons to try to justify not being intimate. This might lead to a heated argument and the possibility of one of you storming out to sleep in another room (which might seem an ideal solution under the circumstances, but doesn't leave either of you feeling very good). It's easy to understand, when breaking down the potential outcome of telling the truth, why you can't really be blamed for wanting to rely on a simple excuse.

So, excuses may indeed be a short-term solution to avoiding confrontation with your partner. But in the long run, you'll still be bogged down with negative thoughts and angry feelings towards him, and these don't just disappear over time. Instead, they ferment and rot inside of you, creating lots of shit that will constipate your relationship. Instead of feeling completely relaxed in each other's arms, vulnerable and open with one another, you feel restrained and restricted, held back, disconnected and disengaged. If you're hoping to keep your partner for life, fabricating excuses is not a good long-term solution to dealing with the real issues that are keeping you apart.

—

Now that we know what excuses are and why we use them, it's time to move beyond them. It's time to delve into the *real* reasons married couples don't have sex. I'm sure that you will recognize yourself in several of the chapters to follow. In preparation for what is to come, please raise your hand if you:

- won't let your partner see you naked in the light;
- feel that yours has become a platonic relationship;
- feel that you are out of sync with one another or that you are not working as a team;
- no longer like, respect, or feel attracted to the person you feel your partner has become;
- are tired of arguing about the same old things without much change;
- are feeling bored;
- wish that you had dated more before you settled down;
- think that he or she is a lousy lover with little interest in improving things; or
- are finding yourself attracted to others.

If you raised your hand once or more, keep that point (or those points) at the top of your mind. My hope is that after reading the next section of this book, you will be open to discussing your sexual relationship with your spouse in a new and much more healthy way—a way that allows you to stop fabricating excuses and begin enjoying sex and intimacy with one another.

Part II

So Little Sex, So Many Reasons

Four

"Don't Look at Me!"

WHEN IT COMES to the real reasons why married people don't have sex as often as one or both partners might like, feeling self-conscious about one's body is high on the list—especially for women. Many women who struggle with weight issues, for example, may avoid intimacy because they don't want to share or show their bodies to their partners (and may not even like what they see themselves when they catch a glimpse of their bodies in the mirror), so they undress in the bathroom with the door closed, and refuse to be naked with the lights on.

Carlyle Jansen, owner of Good for Her, says that issues related to being self-conscious about one's appearance come up a lot in their workshops—especially in the stripping, burlesque, and orgasm workshops. "If you can't stop thinking about how you look or whether the lights are low enough to hide your imperfections," she says, "then you won't be able to relax into an orgasm."

Weighty Issues

✳ KYLE AND LYNNE ✳

One of the reasons Kyle and Lynne got along so well when they began dating was because they were both adventurous eaters. They loved exploring the different ethnic neighbourhoods in their city and sharing dishes with names they couldn't even pronounce. Lynne even kept journal entries as reminders so they could order their favourites again. So, when Kyle was accepted into culinary school, they were both thrilled that he would be able to experiment in their kitchen too.

Lynne had always struggled with her weight, but Kyle didn't seem to be bothered by this when they were dating. He ate a lot more than she did but, like most men, seemed to metabolize food differently. After the birth of their two children, Lynne struggled with her weight even more. Five years after giving birth to their second child, she still hadn't lost her "baby" weight, despite trying numerous diets. Having Kyle as cook and grocery shopper didn't help. Even though he said he wanted to support her, his actions didn't match his words. Instead of milk, he would often add cream to sauces. Instead of buying the leanest minced meat, he'd choose a pack higher in fat because he said it tasted better.

Often, during dinner, Lynne would catch Kyle looking in her direction as she served herself a dollop of his creamy mashed potatoes or took an extra spoonful of dessert. He didn't need to say anything out loud (his eyes did all the talking), but he often did. Even in front of company or the kids, he'd say things like, "Are you really still hungry?" or "Didn't you say you were watching your weight?" His words always stung and often brought tears to Lynne's eyes. She mostly ignored him, thinking that a response would only draw more attention to his comment. His words brought back memories of her mother, in particular, saying similar things.

Lynne was sure that Kyle had no idea how heavily his words weighed on her. She justified his comments by trying to convince herself that he was only trying to help, but his comments had just the opposite effect. Sometimes, after dinner, while loading dishes into the dishwasher and sweeping the floor, Lynne would check to make sure that Kyle and the kids were occupied before helping herself to something extra, such as a large bowl of ice cream on top of which she poured chocolate sauce. Instead of sitting down to enjoy the treat, she devoured it quickly while standing by the kitchen sink for fear that she would be caught.

Many nights, when Kyle draped his arm over her and tried to draw her closer, Lynne turned away. "Sorry, Kyle, I'm really tired," she'd say. She didn't think that Kyle really cared anyway. She thought, Why would he want to have sex with someone he thinks of as so unattractive anyway?

She answered her own question by deciding that it didn't matter how she looked as long as the lights were out. But thinking that her husband would be just as happy with a plastic doll as he was with her didn't make

Lynne any happier; in fact, it made her even less inclined to be intimate with him.

She'd often lie awake at night, sometimes throwing invisible daggers at the back of his head. Her stomach churned at the thought of fulfilling his sexual needs, all the while not feeling desired by him.

———

Lynne's situation wasn't healthy, but it wasn't until she shared her hidden torment with her best friend—who recommended that she and Kyle come to see me—that she took the important first step toward getting help. Like many women, Lynne was reluctant to expose the real reason she was avoiding sex with Kyle. Nevertheless, she fulfilled her promise to her friend by calling.

When Lynne and Kyle arrived at my office, I knew nothing about them other than that they were "experiencing difficulties" in their relationship. I learned that Lynne worked part-time as a paralegal and enjoyed her job. She shared that she was the eldest of three girls and had been raised by both parents. Growing up, her dad worked long hours and her mom was in charge at home. Mom, she shared, was skinny and petite, as were her two sisters. Lynne was the black sheep—and much more plump. She was jealous of their ability to eat more than she did and not gain any weight. Her mother was critical of her eating habits, and her father affectionately called her his "chunky lamb chop," which usually made everyone else laugh. Not Lynne, though. She was embarrassed and often cried in her room, silently, so no one could hear. At night, when everyone else was asleep, she would sneak downstairs to eat leftovers.

Kyle had grown up as the eldest of two boys. His parents

divorced when he was very young and he couldn't remember them ever living together. He divided his time equally between his mom's and dad's houses. He was athletic at school and won a scholarship to attend university. He dropped out of mechanical engineering after second year, realizing it wasn't for him. He met Lynne at a party. He loved her laugh and the colour of her eyes. He loved that she didn't seem to mind that he hadn't already carved out his career path.

She too was attracted to him immediately. They dated for a couple of years before they decided to live together and eventually marry. Now, ten years and two kids later, they both agreed that they were feeling disconnected. He said that he rarely heard her laugh anymore and that the light had gone out of her eyes. She said yes, she was sad and feeling unloved. He tried to convince her how much he loved her by listing off all the things he did for her, such as taking the boys outside to play so that she could sleep late. Eventually, after a couple of sessions, she managed to muster up the courage to share the real reason she was avoiding having sex with him: she was afraid that he found her fat and unattractive, and that he didn't really "want" her anymore. Kyle was shocked by her disclosure. He tried to tell her how pretty she was, but she was not convinced.

Eventually, Kyle admitted that he did not find her as sexually attractive as he once had. "I feel awful admitting this," he said, "but I can't help what I'm feeling." Tearfully, Lynne thanked him for being honest. She admitted that it was hard to hear the truth but assured him that she understood how he might be feeling this way. Kyle shared that he wasn't interested in her shrinking down to a size 8, and that he certainly understood that bodies change over time, especially after pregnancy, but that he would find her more desirable without the "extra padding."

After helping Kyle realize the impact that his comments and suggestions were having on Lynne, and that his words and actions weren't always in sync, I suggested that they take a break from couples counselling so that Lynne could explore her emotional eating with someone who specialized in the field. The last report I had from Lynne was that the realization of how unhappy she was with her weight was what finally pushed her to do something about it. Once she had put the wheels in motion and noticed changes, she indicated that she was feeling much better about herself, was no longer using food as an emotional crutch, and was feeling more confident. Kyle had stopped making derogatory comments about her food choices, had adjusted his selection of ingredients for the whole family, and was allowing her to take control of her eating habits.

The combination of feeling better about her own body and Kyle's support made a huge difference in Lynne and Kyle's relationship. Lynne was more willing to expose herself emotionally and physically to her husband, and as a result, they were enjoying being more intimate with one another.

Age-Related Changes

* SAMIRA *

Fifty-seven-year-old Samira only stood in front of the mirror naked when she knew that she was alone in the house. She didn't dare expose her changing body to her husband or her kids. When all was quiet, she'd sometimes fantasize about how her body had looked a couple of decades earlier. She'd stand in front of the mirror, cup her breasts in her hands, and lift them up and towards one another, remembering how they were once fuller and perkier. She'd pull the skin taut around her mouth, eyes and under her chin, remembering what she looked like before tiny lines revealed themselves and the loose skin under her chin made her look like a turkey. But the image of her new self—her *real* self—sometimes reared its ugly head when her husband reached for her at night. When he tried to remove her nightgown she'd say she was cold. The excuse was preferable to revealing that she couldn't bear the thought of him touching her sagging breasts.

———————————————————————

Weight-related issues may be the number one concern for women, but age-related changes have to be a close second. Like it or not, our bodies change as we age. Breasts sag, wrinkles appear, our hips and waists may widen, even our hair may thin. Many of us fight these changes with surgery, age-defying creams and serums, Botox injections and fillers. With so many people desperate to stave off sagging skin and wrinkles, dermatologists are spending more time helping their patients remain eternally youthful than ever before. When people make comments such as "You look great! Have you lost weight?" or when we barely recognize well-known television personalities or movie stars because they've had so much "work," we are reminded that our society appears to affirm firm and snub saggy. So it's no wonder that skin tags sprouting like little mushroom stalks, varicose veins, graying hair, and age spots affect how we feel about ourselves.

Some couples mutually agree that smooth, supple skin and a youthful physical appearance are at the top of the list of what makes each attractive to the other, so they may together explore interventions such as Botox or plastic surgery. Where couples get into trouble, however, is when one of the partners gives youthful appearance a higher ranking than the other and wants his or her partner to change in a way that is not comfortable for the other. The person who is being asked to consider Botox injections, for example, may resent and ultimately reject his or her partner for making the request.

This is indeed a delicate topic and one that requires careful consideration and communication. If you've been married for a while, you likely know your partner's views on aging naturally versus intervention. You may know, for example, how he will feel about your request that he colour his graying hair or how she might respond to your suggestion that she consult with a plastic surgeon about breast augmentation. Many partners—especially those who have strong and open channels of communication— may be able to request minor changes without creating a volcanic eruption ("I prefer to look at your face without facial hair. Would you mind getting rid of the beard?"). But even the healthiest of relationships could have trouble standing up to requests for more major changes (such as "Your vagina isn't as tight since you gave birth to the kids. I've heard that there are doctors who can correct that" or "Could you look into hair transplants? I've noticed your hairline receding quite dramatically lately.")

* PLASTIC SURGERY: IS IT REALLY THE SOLUTION? *

Some women who are unhappy with their bodies may turn to plastic surgery. According to plastic and reconstructive surgeon Dr. Martin Jugenburg of the Toronto Cosmetic Surgery Institute, the thing most women are looking to change is breast size. Second on the list is the labia (who knew?), and vaginal tightening is also becoming more popular.

While some women may see an improvement in their sexual experiences once they've made changes to the body parts that they don't like, will this change be permanent and, if so, is going under the knife worth the risk? I've counselled women who initially believed that if only they had larger breasts, for example, their husbands would find them more attractive. Unfortunately, some of these women found that not much changed after they increased their cup size. If you're not compatible—both in and out of bed—or if there are deeper reasons for not wanting or having sex, then a snip, tuck, or extension is not likely going to make a huge difference.

Are Men Self-Conscious Too?

Are men as self-conscious as women are about the way they look? I believe that men do care about what others see, but not to the same extent as women. Dr. Jugenburg agrees: "Women are more self-conscious in front of their partners and men less so or not at all." He works exclusively with women but says that some of his colleagues see men for procedures such as penile enlargements and lengthening, breast reductions and non-surgical procedures such as Botox injections. He believes that men seeking these procedures are likely doing so mostly for themselves, whereas women talk more about feeling that their perceived imperfections are affecting their relationships.

Premature Balding

* MARK *

When I first met Mark he was in his early thirties and married with a child. He had met his wife ten years earlier and they married in their mid-twenties. She remembers him shaving his head during their honeymoon because he was conscious of his receding hairline and didn't want others to notice it too. By shaving his entire head of hair, he reasoned at the time, there would be uniform baldness rather than thinning here and there. Wherever he went, Mark would compare his hair to other men. He'd think, Why me? when he hung out with his peers, all in their mid-twenties and not showing any obvious signs of hair loss. He was afraid to let his hair grow in because he didn't want to notice more signs of premature balding.

Even though his wife didn't seem to be bothered by his hair loss, he thought of himself as less attractive than he had been with a full head of hair. When his wife told him that she was no longer in love with him and wanted a separation, they came to see me. Even in session, she wasn't able to fully define what had gone wrong; she just stated that she wasn't in love with him anymore. Mark was more convinced than ever that if only he looked different she would love him again.

═══════════════════════════════════

After Mark and his wife parted ways, he made up his mind to do something about his looks. He began doing some research into the reasons for premature balding and its effect on men. He even came across a study that affirmed what he was feeling about his attractiveness to women. It looked at men who had posted two different pictures of themselves on a dating site: one taken when bald and the other with a full head of hair. The study counted the number of responses from women and concluded that the "hair" pictures received many more responses. For Mark, this sealed the deal. He began a hair restoration process that involved transplanting donor tissue from areas where hair growth was thick to areas where it was sparse. When Mark returned to my office on his own several years after being divorced, I barely recognized him. I asked if he was happier with his new look. He said yes, but admitted that he had now become consumed with worry that he would run out of areas with thick hair (as these too thinned over time) to "donate" to larger areas of balding. Even though he was quick to tell me that he was not suffering from body dysmorphic disorder (I hadn't even asked!), I encouraged him to consider exploring ways to accept this genetic predisposition and to work on alternate thoughts with which to replace the negative, obsessive ones.

Men Who Feel Fat

Of all our perceived and actual bodily imperfections, concern about being overweight should be one of the more easy to remedy. Stereotypically, women are more conscious of their weight—perhaps thanks to the svelte women we see on television shows and movies and in the pages of magazines (often Photoshopped to look that way!). It's no surprise, then, that there are weight loss programs aplenty for us. As it turns out, though, jolly old Santa Claus with his potbelly may also not be as jolly and confident as he appears.

---

* CHARLES AND JACKIE *

When Charles, aged thirty-five, and his thirty-four-year-old wife, Jackie, first came to see me, he was recovering from a heart attack. She asked him to join her in counselling after reading and relating well to my most recent co-authored book, *How Can I Be Your Lover When I'm Too Busy Being Your Mother?* He agreed. She told him that she wanted to make changes in the way they shared responsibilities at home.

She disclosed that since his heart attack, in addition to working part-time outside the house, and carting the kids to and from school and extracurricular activities, she was literally and figuratively doing all of the heavy lifting at home while Charles rested up. At least, she said, he had taken the kids to school before his medical crisis. In addition to being physically exhausted, Jackie was feeling emotionally frustrated and depleted.

What began as concern about division of chores ultimately led to her expressing concern about Charles's unhealthy lifestyle, which included inactivity and weight concerns. He admitted that his weight (more than three hundred pounds) slowed him down, but he didn't appear concerned about the negative impact that this was having on himself and his family. Jackie, on the other hand, was feeling panicked. She envisioned the worst-case scenario if he didn't make changes. In the short term, she said that his weight was impacting his ability to keep up with the kids, his ability to help around the house, and their sex life. Ultimately, with my help, she was able to express her concerns, and he was able to hear them. At one point, when she talked about how she missed having a more physical relationship with him (he had gained a considerable amount of weight since they married, which affected her desire to be with him and his ability to perform), he cried and resolved to work towards becoming healthier and more involved. As soon as he was ready for change, I was able to guide them towards their goals.

Charles's story helps us see how men and women deal differently with issues around being overweight. Most women feel that you can't be both fat and sexy (and those who feel differently are often fetishized), which explains their discomfort with disrobing in front of their husbands in the light. These women often tell therapists like me that they want to lose weight so they can look better and feel better, both in bed and out. Men, on the other hand, don't talk about wanting to lose weight for the same reasons. Sure, they may be self-conscious when they're younger and dating, but when they're married, they don't feel the need to undress in the dark. They may be aware of strangers' stares at an outdoor pool, may feel down on themselves for not fixing their weight problem, but they won't avoid sex for the same reasons overweight women will.

Some of the real reasons (according to what I've heard from weight loss guru Harvey Brooker and my own clients) that overweight men are likely not having sex are because:

- They lack the energy to get off the couch.
- They're being rejected by their wives, who are no longer physically attracted to them (and I'm told may sometimes even be "repulsed" by them as they get fatter).
- They're sleeping in a separate room because the excess pounds are causing them to snore and their wives have banished them.
- They're wearing a Darth Vader–like CPAP (continuous positive airway pressure) mask over their mouths to prevent sleep apnea.
- The extra weight they are carrying is preventing them from being able to achieve positions that enable penetration of their partner.
- They're feeling down on themselves, their self-confidence is in the toilet, and, because of their mental state, they've lost the desire for sex.

I'm not saying that overweight women are immune to sleep apnea, snoring, or a lack of energy, for example, but these are not the most common reasons they list when asked why they are not having or avoiding sex with their spouses.

Harvey Brooker's weight loss program, designed specifically for men, has been active for more than twenty-five years. Brooker says that the thousands of sexuality surveys that he has men fill out anonymously—before and after their weight loss—are proof positive that the majority of his members are not having sex when they're fat. Most say that they're getting zero sex when they first come in, but after they've lost weight, they are more attractive to their wives and have a lot more energy and stamina for sexual activity.

What happens if you have two overweight people married to one another? Well, if only one person wants to work towards a healthier lifestyle, which may include losing weight, the relationship is going to become lopsided—both literally and figuratively.

* DAVID AND JIM *

David and Jim are both losers, but I'm sure they wouldn't have it any other way. David has been married to his wife for twenty years, and Jim to his for fourteen. David said that when he began his journey towards losing weight, his wife was pessimistic. According to David, she had seen him lose and gain his weight back several times and thought that the Harvey Brooker weight loss program he was investing in was a waste of time and money. Despite this, he was bound and determined to lose weight. He even purchased a second fridge for their basement so that he didn't have to see or eat the food she bought for the rest of the family. Six months and eighty pounds lighter, what he's lost in weight, he's gained in self-esteem, confidence, and health.

Jim, who lost 178 pounds in fourteen months, said that when he first began his radical change in lifestyle and eating, his wife felt left behind emotionally and physically. She couldn't keep up with him and felt like she wasn't a part of his life anymore. Once he recognized this, about a year into the process, he worked at involving her. They began walking down the same path by exercising together and eating more of the same foods. Inspired by her husband, she's lost over fifty pounds too. Since working at and supporting one another while losing weight, they've continued to explore other ways to connect—by learning to play guitar and then sharing their newfound skills while singing at local karaoke events together.

Both men see their weight loss as the beginning of a whole new lease on life.

You can see the benefits of having a spouse who ultimately supports and believes in you. However, sometimes both men and women feel unsupported in their weight loss efforts or feel that they are being sabotaged by spouses who tempt them with delectable goodies or discourage them from receiving outside support. Why would this be? Well, when a husband is overweight, a wife knows that other women are less likely to find him attractive. Or perhaps the husband is worried about losing his buffet buddy or having her, newly enlightened and reformed about what's healthy and not, imposing her will on him, even though he knows he also has weight to lose. Or maybe one spouse is not ready to commit to a healthier lifestyle and resents the other's "holier than thou" attitude about what's best.

One thing is for certain, though. When it comes to body image issues—whether weight-related, age-related or other, and whether experienced by men or women—permanent change only works when the desire comes from within. Being forced to adopt a different lifestyle doesn't work, and doing something because you want to be healthier or slimmer for someone else is not a good thing either.

✳ HARVEY BROOKER ✳

More than forty years ago, Harvey Brooker, then a twenty-seven-year-old husband and father, began his journey towards a healthier lifestyle. Harvey was twelve years old when his father died at the age of forty-eight. And, like his father, Harvey was a two-pack-a-day smoker until he told himself, Keep this up and you won't be around to see your grandchildren. So he quit smoking, lost fifty pounds, and has maintained his weight loss and healthy lifestyle promise to himself and his family.

When he's not enjoying life with wife, Helen, his grown kids, and seven grandkids, Harvey's a sought-after mentor and guide to thousands of men who have followed his lead and flock to his meetings. The Harvey Brooker weight loss program for men is a one-of-a-kind worldwide phenomenon.

Is This You?

Are worries about your appearance getting in the way of a healthy sexual relationship between you and your partner? Read and think about the following statements. You can even put a checkmark next to the ones that describe your feelings.

- I remove my clothes in the dark, under the covers, or behind closed doors.
- I don't want to be on top because I'm too heavy.
- I don't want to have sex with the lights on because my body's imperfections will be too noticeable.
- I'd rather not shower together.
- I prefer not to kiss when we're having sex in case my breath smells bad.

Okay, now let's look at those checkmarks. Are there three or more? If so, it's likely that your sex life is being affected by your negative self-image.

First Steps to Talk It Out

So now what? Well, having identified the problem, you are in a much better position to deal with it. Keep in mind that if you'd prefer that your partner not look at you naked, you are likely communicating this through non-verbal clues. However, your partner may misinterpret the message and believe that you are no longer interested in him. If you are feeling self-conscious, the first step is to let your partner know what you are thinking and feeling. So, for example, instead of waiting until you are in bed together, ask him (at another quiet time) if he ever worries about your seeing him naked and then, following his response, let him know what you are feeling self-conscious about and why. This way, there are no secrets and he will understand, and maybe even help you overcome, your need to wear your nightgown when you're making love.

But what if you are feeling less desirous of your partner as a result of something related to his body? Again, clear communication is the key. Be honest but kind. Say something like, "I've noticed that you don't seem to be showering as much lately. Sometimes, when we are intimate, I'm turned off by your body odour. I'm wondering if you'd mind showering more regularly." Be open to your partner's being defensive or hurt at first. Ultimately, though, once your partner has heard and understood your feelings, he may need time to digest your words and decide what (if anything) he is going to do differently. If he chooses not to change, then at least he will do so knowing how it impacts you individually, and how it may impact you as a couple.

If the change in physical attraction is ascribed to something that cannot be controlled—such as balding or age spots—or to a physical attribute that has been constant since you met—such as breast size—then I do not recommend trying to have an honest discussion about this. It might be helpful, however, to work through this problem yourself—with the help of a therapist or by reading self-help books and articles. In the process, you may find, for example, that your discomfort at seeing your partner's body changing is related more to your fear of aging or mortality than to anything else.

Five

The Roommate Syndrome

WHAT DO YOU share in common? When I ask couples this question, it is often followed by a period of silence, sometimes followed by "Our kids?!" Strangely, this is not something most couples think about. Most do have things in common when they first meet, and this is part of what initially connects them, but over the years, those common interests fall away, and are sometimes replaced by separate outside interests. Couples who have been married for a long time—who perhaps have children and mortgages and busy lives—often express sadness and regret over the fact that they haven't kept in touch with each other—over things other than the kids. There can be a feeling of disconnectedness, of having little in common. Some describe the sensation as being out of sync, or like two ships passing in the night. Often, these couples do a top-notch job of keeping it all together; they manage a family and their own lives very well, but underneath it all, there can be a feeling of emptiness or loss. It's a situation I often describe as the "roommate syndrome."

Roommates need to be somewhat compatible in regards to

their personal values and level of tidiness, for example, but they can also shut their bedroom doors and maintain separate lives without any repercussions. That rarely works for married couples; the expectations are different, and the disappointments greater when things don't work out. It's much more difficult to walk away from a marriage than it is from an apartment you share with a friend. To make a marriage work over the long term, a couple needs to be able to merge personal styles, learn the art of compromise, accept and tolerate differences, engage in shared interests regularly, and work together to build on their foundation. Separate interests, separate beds, and separate bank accounts are just some of the telltale signs that you and your spouse are more roommates than lovers.

* SONIA AND SELWYN *

Sonia and Selwyn have been married twenty-eight years. For most of the previous year, their two children have been away at university. During the summer, the kids returned to the nest, but even then they weren't home much of the time. Both husband and wife are professionals. His work as an accountant, and hers as a medical doctor, mean long hours and time away from one another. So, over the years, as they spent less time together as a family during their down time, they drifted apart as a couple. Looking back, each says that they had anticipated this period of time (when the kids left home) with eagerness. They considered the freedom that they'd have to travel more, to go out for spontaneous dinners or walks with their dog without worrying about what time to be home to pick a child up at a friend's house or extracurricular activity. Unfortunately, they said, perhaps as a result of their devotion to their careers and raising children, they hadn't nurtured their relationship over the years. Now that they were able to do the things they had fantasized about, they no longer felt the desire to do so. Instead, Sonia preferred getting together with her friends or going to the gym after work, and Selwyn often didn't return home from work until around 10 p.m. Most nights, Sonia went to bed while Selwyn ate a late dinner in front of the television.

Sonia knew of my practice because we had patients in common, so she reached out for an appointment. During the session, Sonia revealed that she had contacted me after suddenly becoming acutely aware of how lonely and sad she felt in her relationship. I acknowledged that the feeling of loneliness while in a relationship is often more upsetting than what you might feel when living alone; when you're with someone, you know that you shouldn't be feeling this way. She said that she was feeling disconnected from Selwyn, and that she saw him more as a roommate than as her lover. Interestingly, these feelings had been highlighted for her after observing their older daughter in a relationship. Along with being excited that her daughter had found someone to be with, Sonia told me she felt envious that none of the spark and love she saw between the young couple was present in her own relationship.

We talked about the evolution of relationships, and she recognized that changes were normal over time. She understood that the bright spark and intense passion that she saw in her daughter's new relationship might not be a realistic expectation in her own, but I acknowledged her yearning for it and commended her desire and intention to try to get at least some of it back in her marriage.

I suggested that she ask Selwyn to join us at a subsequent session and she agreed to this, along with my recommendation that she give him the choice of coming in one time without her so that he didn't feel that I was biased.

Selwyn declined the one-on-one session but agreed to join Sonia. Together, we continued to explore where they were in their relationship and where they wanted to be. The good news is that they were both on the same page. Selwyn recognized that their relationship had become platonic or even business-like, and that romance, intimacy, and sex had not been a part of their lives in a long time (they agreed that it had been almost a year since they had sex and that they were rarely intimate). Selwyn said that he missed the intimacy even more than the sex. Sonia said that it was difficult to connect with him physically when she felt so disconnected emotionally. We talked about the classic chicken-and-egg cycle: the less contented one feels emotionally, the less likely one is to want to connect physically. And the less one connects physically, the less emotionally connected one feels.

Things Have Changed

If you've been married for a couple of years or more, you know what I mean when I say that sex, in particular, is very different when you're living together or married than when you're dating. Back then, even a hard day's work didn't slow you down. You couldn't wait to jump in the shower, freshen your face, throw on something casually seductive, and enjoy a romantic dinner followed by something delicious—each other. Unfortunately, when we're living together we become lazy. There's always tomorrow evening to go out or do something special, so you throw on a comfy pair of sweatpants and sink into the couch to watch a show on television or escape into another screen on your lap or in your hand. You take for granted that your partner will always be around if you experience a sexual urge, which becomes more and more rare. When you're dating, you make time for one another and for intimacy. Sex is intense. Exciting. Novel. Ironically, when you're living together, spending time as a couple takes more effort. And depending on the number of years that you've been together, sex is more infrequent and less passionate.

Separate Beds

Finding time for healthy, satisfying sex can be a particular challenge if a couple is no longer sharing a bed—a more common occurrence than one might think. A sleep study conducted by researchers at Toronto's Ryerson University found that a surprising 30 to 40 percent of couples sleep apart at night.[1] Some end up sleeping in separate rooms, while others may opt for separate beds in the same room. Perhaps it's a partner's snoring that leads to the new arrangements, or someone's preference for a harder or softer mattress. Whatever the reason, for almost half of all couples, the marital bed may be a thing of the past.

For some, this works. Each gets a better night's rest, and they are both happy with their level of intimacy (maybe even climbing into one or the other's bed for a little fun before saying good night). For the majority, however, this type of sleeping arrangement is a slippery slope towards a relationship where each regards the other as a companion rather than lover.

✳ WHAT HAPPENS WHEN YOU'RE AWAY? ✳

Life at home may be filled with to-do lists and drudgery, but life on vacation is another thing entirely, right? Shouldn't "getting away from it all" with your partner give you the chance to get back to the fun-loving, intimate couple you once were?

Wives often tell me that although they look forward to going on vacations without the kids, it's mostly the break from domestic responsibilities that they are really craving, not necessarily a chance to spend quality time with their spouse. For many women, being alone in a hotel room with their husbands compounds the guilt or pressure they feel to perform. They say that their husbands typically anticipate that sex will be abundant during their time away (after all, there are no kids, chores, or other distractions). However, for a woman, it may take a few days before the stressors of home and the memories of less-pleasant interactions have faded enough to spark interest, and many wives report that desire is not as easy to flip on as a light switch. This often causes conflict and disappointment and may lead to a less-pleasurable vacation than either had anticipated.

My advice is to discuss the elephant in the room before heading away. It can sometimes be helpful if neither partner anticipates having sex during the first couple of days of their vacation. This way, the pressure is off and things don't start on a sour note. If they do end up having sex, it's because they want to, not because anyone feels obligated.

Power Plays

The challenges of living together in a long-term relationship are many and varied. Sonia and Selwyn's example may be the most common—a couple simply drifts apart as the years pass—but it's hardly the only way in which a marriage can experience difficulties from within.

Business Partners

Some couples, for example, literally work together, as in she's his bookkeeper or he's her IT guy. For many, keeping it in the family has its advantages—lots of time spent together, a sense of shared purpose, and so on. However, if one partner's position is perceived by either as greater or lesser than the other, the dynamics in their relationship can become unhealthy. They won't be able to see themselves as a balanced team and this perception can spill over into the bedroom. So, for example, if she's feeling condescended to or less important, she may (subconsciously, even) attempt to assert more power and control by refusing his sexual advances. In general, one or both may find it difficult to compartmentalize their roles. So, instead of being able to hang up their professional hats at the door, so to speak, they continue to play their work roles outside working hours. This may perpetuate their perception of each other as working or business partners rather than romantic lovers.

That disconnected feeling can also occur when one partner or the other brings a little too much of the office home. A successful lawyer may receive kudos in the workplace for the way in which she dispenses advice to clients who admire and respect her and are seeking her input, but advice giving may not be appreciated by her spouse, who would prefer she simply listen and empathize rather than tell him what to do. Or a respected police sergeant might need to recognize that the way in which he runs a tight ship at the station and delegates tasks to his officers is perhaps not the best approach at home with his wife, who wants him by her side as her partner, not her superior. Although it may be difficult to accept that characteristics that have been encouraged in one environment may be intolerable in another, most husbands and wives are willing to explore this in an effort to create more of a connection at home.

Money Matters

Money is high on the list of contentious and divisive issues for most couples. In fact, a recent eHarmony survey revealed that "money matters" was second only to "free time" on the list of things couples argue about most. I am always curious to learn about the way in which a couple manages their finances. My belief is that this is often reflective of other dynamics in the relationship. For example, if a husband and wife maintain strictly separate bank accounts—with no joint account for household expenses—I see a red flag. I have to wonder what else is going on. Is there a power imbalance? Are there trust issues? Is one partner hiding transactions they don't want the other to see? Is someone secretly stashing away some savings, just in case things "don't work out"? In some cases, it may be that each is responsible for a different set of household bills. So, he might manage the mortgage and other household utility bills, such as hydro and gas, while she manages groceries and school supplies with hers. Or they might even split the rent, as roommates typically do.

For some couples—especially those who maintain complete transparency and access to each other's account (that is, knowledge of how much each is depositing and withdrawing on a regular basis)—this system works. For the majority, however, the division of financial responsibilities and keeping separate (and sometimes even secret) bank accounts can lead to that troublesome "roommate" feeling. There's something about a joint bank account, with complete disclosure, that suggests more of a unified, connected approach to walking through life as a team.

A word of caution (and explanation): merely merging your accounts will not transform your relationship from roommates to lovers. Before you rush to the bank in search of a quick fix, take some time to consider why your lives are divided in this way and what you can do to bridge the gap.

Is This You?

Do you feel like you're living with a friend rather than a lover? Is the passion you once felt for each other a distant memory? Consider the following statements and check off the ones that apply to you:

- The most contact we have is when we sit down each week to sync our calendars and go over the bills that need to be paid.

- He does all the outside work. I do all the indoor stuff. It's rare that we work together.
- We split most of the household finances.
- We have separate bathrooms, separate closets, and separate shelves in the fridge.
- We feel a little awkward when we have the opportunity to be physically intimate with one another.

Did you end up with three or more checkmarks? If so, it's likely that you and your spouse are feeling more like roommates or business partners than lovers.

First Steps to Compatibility Circles

This exercise provides you and your spouse with an opportunity to remember and think about what connected you to one another when you first met and what connects you now.

Can you picture a Venn diagram? It consists of two circles that partially overlap in the middle. You and your partner are going to create one that describes your relationship. First, find a time that works for both of you—either at home or on a "date" at a restaurant, coffee shop, or somewhere else you can talk. Then, using an 8.5 x 11-inch sheet of unlined paper, draw your two overlapping circles. Over the top of the circle on the left, write *His Interests*; write *Her Interests* over the top of the circle on the right. Over the overlapping section, write—you guessed it—*Our Interests*.

Creating the diagram is the easy part. The hard part—or at least the "thinking" part—is filling in the circles. For example, he may list going for walks, watching sports on TV, trying out new restaurants, watching the kids at gymnastics, and playing golf with the guys in his circle. She may list watching reality TV, working out at the gym, playing mah-jongg with friends, going skating as a family, and going to live theatre in hers. The most revealing part of this exercise is what happens in the *Our Interests* section. In other words, how much do you have in common, or how compatible are you?

Sometimes, finding common ground takes a bit of work. Based on the interests detailed above, the couple completing their compatibility circles might worry that they don't have a lot in common. But things may not be as dire as they first appear. Consider, for example:

- He prefers golf and going for walks; she prefers working out at the gym and going skating. Nevertheless, *staying active* can absolutely be listed as a joint interest.

- She enjoys watching reality TV; he prefers live sports. Still, "watching TV" is a joint interest.

- She enjoys live theatre and he enjoys trying out new restaurants, but they both enjoy going out.

- She has listed "going skating as a family" while he has listed "watching the kids at gymnastics." A common interest may be "making the kids feel special."

- He likes playing golf with friends and she prefers mah-jongg, but they both value "time spent away from one another with friends."

You can see how even different interests may be grouped together under the same umbrella. By identifying common interests, a couple may feel closer and may even learn something about one another. In addition, this exercise can serve as a springboard for discussion. She may suggest that they combine interests and go to dinner and a play together one evening. Or perhaps he could take out a trial membership at the gym while she agrees to a few golf lessons.

Unfortunately, not every couple will emerge from this experience with a positive reaffirmation of shared interests. For some, the exercise will serve as a wakeup call—a visual reminder that they do not currently share enough in common and thus need to work towards finding more things to include in the overlapping section.

As an extension of this exercise, consider also creating compatibility circles for *When We Met* and *Where We Are Now*. This might remind you about the things that first drew you together, and help you identify what parts of your relationship you may wish to recapture.

Six

All Stressed Out

W E'RE ALL FAMILIAR with the stereotype of the stressed-out wife—too busy with the kids, the house, and perhaps her own job outside the house to have time or energy left over for intimacy. The thing about stereotypes, of course, is that they have a basis in reality. Women's lives have changed radically since the 1950s, for example, when her main "job" was to make sure that her home was tidy, her children were well behaved, and there was a hot meal or a cold drink waiting for hubby when he got home from a hard day at the office.

Given the demands placed on women today—in a world where women want and have worked hard for successful careers of their own; and where parenting all too often has become a competitive activity—is it any wonder that women feel stressed and overburdened, and that this might have an effect on a marriage? In previous chapters, we've talked about how some of the feelings unleashed by this constant stress can come into play in the bedroom: being too tired may be her reality, and being angry and frustrated at a lack of help from one's spouse can indeed be a major turn-off. It's safe to say that this type of stress and pressure is likely a factor in any modern marriage, even the most healthy.

Recognizing that, I'd like to spend time in this chapter talking about another kind of stress—the type that comes from expectations and pressure about having sex (whether real or imagined). For many women, especially those who grew up feeling that sex is a duty that must be fulfilled, this type of stress can be very difficult to handle.

The Wifely Duty

In his remarkable 1965 play *Belles-soeurs*, Canadian playwright Michel Tremblay offers his audiences a glimpse into the lives of several middle-class Montreal women in the early 1960s. Germaine Lauzon has won a million trading stamps from a department store and has enlisted fourteen friends to help paste the stamps into booklets that, when filled, will allow her to refurbish and decorate her home with merchandise from the store's catalogue. The women talk as they paste, and speak directly to the audience in engaging monologues: about marriage, about stupid slob husbands who demand sex twice a day, 365 days a year, come hell or high water, and about how they don't want their own daughters to end up the same way they have.

Through the women's dialogues and monologues, we catch a glimpse into the lives of women in this era. Tremblay must either have eavesdropped on many conversations between the adult women in his life or researched his subject well, because his depiction of women unsatisfied by their domestic servitude—including raising kids single-handed and then having to be sexually dutiful, sometimes even twice a day—is painfully accurate.

Fast-forward fifty years and, thankfully, most women have come a long way from the days when their mothers and aunts and grandmothers spread their legs because they felt it was their duty to do so. Now women are encouraged instead to spread their wings and assert themselves in every way, including in the bedroom. One of the biggest social changes over the past half century is that women now have just as important and financially lucrative positions as do their male counterparts. As a result, they feel less honour-bound to prove their worth or play their part within a marriage by having sex whenever their husband wants it. I have noticed, however, that even though there has been great progress towards equality in and out of the bedroom, women still sometimes struggle with these feelings of inequality, especially women who may not work outside the home. Perhaps they feel that because they are not earning an income, they are not pulling their weight, and so feel more obligated to keep the house in good working order. Perhaps they feel pressure—sometimes self-imposed but sometimes external—to keep their children well groomed and disciplined. Perhaps they also feel a duty to "perform" even when they'd rather not.

It's interesting to note that a sense of fear can take root alongside the sense of duty. Women who feel that they need to "earn their keep" by meeting their husband's sexual needs may also fear that he will "go elsewhere" if she doesn't fulfill those needs. If a woman has not carved out her own career path or has devoted herself to staying at home to raise children and keep a clean home, the threat can seem very real. The resulting fear alone may cause her to give in to his sexual demands.

Backed into a Corner

The problem with having sex just because you feel you have to—whether out of a sense of duty or fear—is that it usually doesn't feel good. When someone feels backed into a corner, when sex is not between two consenting adults or between two people who are making love as an expression of their good feelings towards one another, then the act feels empty, a chore, something to be gotten out of the way. And there's certainly no positive glow, no cuddling or kissing. Instead, there's likely another reason to feel resentful at not having one's own feelings considered, another reason to feel less important.

When one partner in a relationship feels that his or her feelings don't count, or that he or she is less important, then resentment, anger and hostility can build over time. Eventually, their sexual relationship becomes robotic and perfunctory and distant from the warmth or positive regard they once felt for one another.

What I have seen in my practice is that women who have higher positive self-regard, who feel that they are equal or bring worth to the relationship (not always financially but in other ways too) are much more likely to push back or pull away from sex when they don't want to engage in it with their partners. If they feel forced into having sex, they tell me, it's more likely that they won't want to. In fact, it's a big turn-off. Men, on the other hand, will often say that it seems as if women always feel backed into a corner—and that they use this as an excuse for getting out of having sex.

Let's explore the dance between these couples that has her backing up and him advancing, even in the face of her evasive moves. Is he not picking up her cues? Is she not being explicit enough, and therefore leaving him feeling confused by her response to his advances? Does he not know how to accept "no"? Does she say no so often that he continues to advance in spite of her resistance, hoping that she will eventually give in?

I have worked with couples in this situation on more than one occasion. By the time they come to see me, it's not unusual for her to be feeling tired, angry, or frustrated as a result of holding him at arm's length. Often, he too is frustrated, angry, and hurt at feeling rejected and undesirable. What has led to this state—her back up against the wall, arms outstretched to push him away, and him pursuing her despite her resistance to his advances?

When He Feels Undesired

What I hear most often from these men is that they feel they are no longer desired, no longer loved. In answer to this, women will often provide lots of examples to show why this belief is not valid. They will remind their husbands of all the things they do to show caring: packing him a lunch every day, reminding him of his doctor's appointment, preparing a meal that she knows he will enjoy. He will nod his head and agree that she does indeed show caring in this way, but will then remind her that he can pay a housekeeper to do all of that. He will share that this kind of caring alone does not make him feel desired. He will say that what he wants—more than packed lunches and reminders—is to have her initiate some of their lovemaking. This, he says, will show him that she still finds him attractive, desirable, that he's someone she considers worthy of having an intimate relationship with. It is his need to feel loved and desired that keeps him pursuing her, in the hopes that he will be reassured that their relationship is still good.

For many men, a decline or loss of a sexual relationship or intimacy with their wife signals the end of their relationship—and it raises lots of fear and anxiety for both partners. He worries that she is going to leave him. He worries that she is attracted to others. He typically doesn't think a lot about how her anger, resentment, and hurt play into her not wanting to have sex. Why? Because all too often, men don't seem to be able to relate to this. Men are typically able to divorce themselves from an argument that took place the day before. They can become physically aroused and ready for action regardless of previous negative exchanges. The majority of men are more than willing to set their differences aside in order to have their sexual needs met. The reason why John Gray's *Men Are from Mars and Women Are from Venus* is such a popular book is because it brings the obvious to light: men and women think and function differently. Sometimes, what seems so obvious to her—that she can't stand the sight of him and certainly doesn't want to caress him or give her body to him after he's said something mean and hurtful—is not at all obvious to him. A negative exchange of words and the desire to have sex are two very separate items to him, and are filed in two very separate compartments of his brain. For her, not so.

Looking for Reassurance

So, he pursues her—looking for reassurance of his desirability—even though her actions make him believe that he is not desired. What he doesn't realize is that she may still find him attractive, desirable, that he may still turn her on, but not now, not today. Instead of sharing this with him—as in "I am so turned off by the way you undermined me in front of the kids that I just can't let you close right now"—she just backs away. Often she makes excuses ("I'm too tired tonight" or "I have a headache"). He knows that this may not be true, and he might either respond with anger or sigh in resignation. Either way, he doesn't really understand why she doesn't want to have sex.

What I have heard from couples over and again is that after several years of repeated conflict between them—never spoken about or resolved, but swept under the rug—and after years of him advancing and her pushing him away, he stops trying. He may retreat behind closed doors to pleasure himself as he watches porn on the Internet. He may seek out other relationships. Or he may just accept what is and live with it—unhappily.

What Is He Thinking?

But let's step back a bit to explore some of the questions I posed a little earlier on—questions related to this viciously repetitive dance.

Firstly, is he not picking up on her cues? Well, he may very well be picking up her cues of disinterest but may be choosing to persist despite the suggestion that she does not want to be close to him. This may be a throwback to a very old-fashioned and sexist belief that even when women say no, they really mean yes, that they might just be playing hard to get. This belief was and still is unfounded and untrue. When women, or men, say no, they should be taken literally—especially when it comes to sex. When a person is forced to have sex without consent, this is rape, plain and simple.

Is she not being explicit enough in her response? Is he confused? Perhaps. Maybe he has had sex with a headache and found that his headache actually improved. He may legitimately believe that he is doing her a favour by helping to distract or rid her of pain, or that sex will help relieve some of her stress. The same may be true when she says she is tired. He perhaps recalls a time when he too was tired but then became aroused when she got into bed and curled her body around his. Suddenly his brain was on high alert and his penis responded accordingly. He would never say no to sex, even if he was tired! So, yes—perhaps she is not being explicit enough to cut through his own thinking on the subject. Maybe she really does need to spell it out so that he understands specifically how their earlier disagreement, or the fact that he hasn't showered for a few days, or that she's feeling particularly unsexy that night is impacting her desire to be close to him.

Does he not know how to accept no? Perhaps he grew up in an environment with very few boundaries. He might have gotten used to eventually getting what he wanted, even though he had been told no at first. Or perhaps he's used to having his wishes granted the minute he asked (or even before he asked) for something. If so, patience might be a foreign concept to him, and he might even respond with a temper tantrum when he hears no. His needs come first. As easy as it might be for him to blame his parents for not teaching him to delay gratification, for giving in to him even when he wasn't very nice, or for spoiling him by giving in to his every desire, it's time for him to accept personal responsibility for his behaviour. You are not his mother and are entitled to ask him to wait or to understand why you are saying no. He may also need to take responsibility for how his actions or words have affected you. If he isn't open to growing up and learning how his behaviour affects others, then the issues in your relationship may go far beyond what happens in the bedroom.

Does she say no so often that he continues to advance in spite of her resistance, in the hope that she will eventually give in? Maybe he believes that his persistence and playful, flirtatious ways will melt her icy exterior. Maybe he feels that he has the power to turn stone into putty. Maybe he figures he has nothing to lose since she says no so often. Maybe he feels challenged by her locked-tight position and sees it as an opportunity for conquest?

A No-Win Situation

Whatever the reason behind his failure to back off, the outcome is typically not good—for the short or the long term. In the moment, he may actually "win" her over. She may have sex with him, but it's likely because she wants him off her back, so to speak, until next time. Or she may comply because she wants to avoid repeated conflict. Either way, it's unlikely that the sex will be loving or passionate or tender or even satisfying. This was confirmed in a 2013 University of Toronto study that found that having sex in order to avoid conflict leads to a less satisfying sexual experience for both partners, and to resentment that impacts the relationship over time.[1]

On the other hand, if he doesn't win her over, he will feel defeated, rejected, unloved, undesired. With either outcome, the long-term results are not good. Both partners will feel a greater disconnect. Neither will feel as if his or her feelings have been taken into account. Each might feel misunderstood and uncared for.

As with so many other problems between couples, the solution here is for each partner to clearly communicate their true feelings and needs. Only after they understand and appreciate the stress, fear, and anxiety each may be feeling can they begin to work on their sex life and intimacy.

Is This You?

In some cases, the stress people feel when it comes to having sex is the garden-variety type that comes with living in the twenty-first century. But sometimes there's something bigger at work. Consider the following statements, and check off any that apply to you.

- I often have sex out of a sense of obligation or duty.
- I feel guilty when we haven't had sex in a long time, so sometimes give in.
- I wonder if my partner is engaging in other sexual relationships or might leave ours someday because of our lack of sex.
- I often feel backed into a corner.
- I wonder if my partner still finds me desirable and attractive.

If you checked off three or more statements, it's likely that stress and fear may be having a negative impact on your relationship.

First Steps to Understanding Personal Space

This exercise is about understanding one another's need for space, and about the non-verbal cues that we often use to communicate that need. For the majority of individuals, the amount of physical distance maintained between oneself and another person is determined by the nature of your relationship and the state of your relationship at the time. In other words, you may feel less comfortable with someone you have just met being so close that you can smell his breath but might be absolutely okay with your lover being in that same close proximity. Even with someone that you are close to, a need for increased personal space can emerge in the aftermath of a fight, or when you are feeling pressured to do something you don't want to do.

Reading another person's non-verbal cues is an essential part of communication. When I'm counselling, for example, it's not just words that I am listening to. I like to note if a couple sit on the same couch or separate, whether their legs are touching or if they're holding hands. I observe whether one reaches out to the other, especially when he or she is in distress, and when one is visibly comfortable in the other's presence or when he or she backs away.

During the following at-home exercise, you will be guided towards becoming more aware of your comfort at having your partner physically close, and also more aware of the non-verbal cues you are sending and receiving. Read through this exercise completely before beginning, as you may want to take note of the kinds of things you will be talking about once the active part of the exercise is complete.

To begin, stand at opposite ends of a room, facing one another.

Then, take one average-sized step towards the other. Stop for about five seconds to observe yourself and your partner in relation to one another. After the first step or two, you will likely be too far apart to feel any discomfort about your space being encroached upon. Continue taking steps towards one another at the same time, stopping after each new step to observe your emotional response to the dynamics between the two of you. When you are about four or five steps away from one another, you are likely to feel a different vibration. By the time you are two or three steps apart, you will likely either feel the desire to stop or to continue so that you are eventually touching one another.

When either you or your spouse reaches the point at which you want to stop moving towards the other, that person can say "Stop." The other person, regardless of whether he or she wants to continue moving forward or not, needs to respect that command.

At this point, each partner has the opportunity to say why they asked for the exercise to stop. She may say something like, "This is the space I feel comfortable with when we are going about our separate lives in the middle of the day." He might say, "But I was hoping you'd come a little closer." She might respond, "If I come closer, will you assume that we have to have sex, or would it be okay for us just to kiss?" If he says, "Kissing is fine," then she might change her mind and agree to move closer. Once they are closer, it would be important for him to respect her desire to just kiss.

This exercise can be repeated over and over. At different times, your desire for connection with one another will change, depending on the state of your relationship and what else is going on around you. It may be interesting and informative for each partner to learn how the boundaries change depending on what else is going on between them and in their world at the time.

This exercise provides you both with an opportunity to spring-board into a verbal discussion about how each was feeling before, during, and after the exercise. Again, the discussion will likely be quite different depending on when the exercise is carried out.

Some questions that might lead to a deeper understanding of each other include:

- Did you have any concerns before we began this exercise? If so, what were they?
- At what point along the way did you notice a change in what you were feeling in regards to our distance or closeness?

- What non-verbal cues did you pick up from me as an indicator that I was reluctant or desirous to continue advancing?
- Why do you think I was feeling this way?

Trying to understand your partner's motivation for distance or closeness will encourage empathy and support towards one another and make both of you feel more understood. If your partner doesn't have a clue as to why you were feeling as you did, take the opportunity to really explain yourself. Try not to place blame on your partner, as this will close the door to effective communication between you. Ask: Is this a pattern that we have seen in our relationship outside of this exercise? If so, explore why this may be.

Seven

Seeing Red

AT THE TOP of the list of all the *real* reasons that couples (especially women) share for not wanting to have sex or be intimate are anger, resentment, and frustration. For some, it's anger or frustration based on an earlier (in the day) interaction; for others, it may be chronic. The negative feelings may simmer just below the surface of the relationship—perhaps as a result of an unrelenting series of repeated patterns of behaviour—often erupting when triggered by a specific event.

---

* MIRIAM AND TREVOR *

Miriam and Trevor have been married for seven years and have twin girls, aged five. Before the girls were born, Miriam was putting her marketing degree to good use at a large company and contributing an equal amount of income to their household budget. After the twins were born, she took her maternity leave while Trevor continued to work. At the end of that year, Trevor suggested hiring a nanny so Miriam could return to her job. Not wanting to leave her post as a stay-at-home mom, Miriam told her husband that she'd prefer to remain at home and continue with their weekly cleaning lady rather than hire someone to take care of their children. Trevor was on board with this, with the understanding that once the girls were old enough to go to school full-time, Miriam would return to work.

That time had come and gone when they came to speak to me about feeling disconnected. They both agreed that sexual intimacy had changed ever since Miriam's belly grew too large for them to be comfortable having sex. And after the babies were born, all of their time—especially Miriam's—was devoted to the twins' needs. Trevor buried his head in work, and often found it tough to easily make ends meet. He resented Miriam's current schedule, which included going to the gym every day and meeting friends for lunch. Frustrated at her for not fulfilling her end of their agreement, he used every opportunity to mention it—sometimes when they were alone and other times in the company of friends. He'd refer to Miriam as "a lady of leisure," or "a kept woman," and would make derogatory comments such as, "What do you do with yourself all day while the kids are at school?" or "Aren't you tired of doing nothing with your life?" Try as she might to convince him that she had plenty to occupy her time, the least of which was spent on her personal needs, he didn't seem to hear her. Instead, he remained angry at her for not contributing to their financial responsibilities. For her part, Miriam felt that Trevor didn't value her contributions to their family's well-being. Every time they tried to share their feelings, they would run into difficulties. Over time, the combination of child-rearing, leading separate lives, and feelings such as resentment, anger, and frustration had driven a wedge between them.

Despite this, Trevor continued to try to connect with his wife, often attempting to pull her towards him in bed at night. But Miriam had a difficult time putting aside their differences in order to have sex, let alone engage in foreplay.

Despite all the layers present in Trevor and Miriam's story, the underlying issues were anger, resentment, and frustration on both sides. I told them that until they had resolved their conflict about when or if she was going to return to work, it was unlikely that sexual intimacy would return. It wasn't that Miriam didn't want foreplay to lead to intercourse; she just wasn't feeling soft or tender or passionate towards her husband, and as we learned earlier, it's hard for women, in particular, to feel intimate when they are not feeling connected.

Sometimes, as with Trevor and Miriam, the reasons for the anger, resentment, and frustration are close to the surface and easy to spot. Other times, however, the underlying causes of these negative feelings can be hard to unearth. I once counselled a couple—Aviva and Ryan—who had been married for twenty-four years when she emailed me to say that they were looking for someone to help them through a rough patch in their relationship. She initially requested that I see her on her own but then emailed me the day before her appointment to ask if it would be okay if her husband joined her. I was fine either way.

My initial impression of Aviva was that she was very good at holding everything together. She arrived with the intake forms I had emailed them in a crisp new purple file folder. The information that I requested had been typed as opposed to handwritten (which is more typical) on the appropriate lines and signed by both her and Ryan. I commented that she appeared well organized and she nodded in validation of my assessment. Aviva's appearance also suggested careful attention to detail: her hair was very neatly arranged, as were her clothing and makeup.

Ryan also was well groomed. His hair was curly and shoulder length. He was wearing a leather jacket, a short-sleeved shirt, and a pair of jeans. He reminded me of someone you might see on a motorcycle, or a musician from a rock band.

They took a few moments deciding whether to sit on one of the two couches together or to each sit on a separate couch or chair. Eventually they settled on a couch each, kitty-corner to one another.

As I always do prior to plunging into the reason a couple has requested a session with me, I asked each to share a little about their personal lives. I find it so important to know about each partner's family of origin, and I like to hear about their siblings and parents, where they were born and raised, whether there is a history of mental health issues in their family, a little about their education, and how they earn a living, if they do. I also ask about whether or not they have children and, if so, something about each of their kids. By the time we get around to the reason for their visit, I have a pretty decent picture of what makes each partner tick, their lives prior to meeting one another, and how they met.

I ask each partner how I can help and what needs to change in order for the problem to be improved. I'm listening to hear if they're on the same page; I'm looking for body language that contradicts their words; and I'm checking to see if they share the desire to make things work or if one has come only to appease the other.

When I asked Aviva how I could help, she told me that although she and Ryan had a great relationship in all other ways, they were struggling with "intimacy." Before turning to Ryan for his input, I wanted to define what she meant, since "intimacy" is such a huge umbrella. From what she shared, it didn't sound like intimacy per se was the issue, since I heard that they were quite comfortable being in close proximity to one another, holding hands, kissing, and even showering together often. What seemed to be the real issue was a lack of sex and a loss of sexual desire on her part.

Ryan confirmed that the loss of sex in their relationship was why he had agreed to come to the session. He told me that he and Aviva had not had sex for at least six months and that he was beginning to feel as if he too might be losing sexual desire. He said he still found his wife physically attractive, but that he had begun to see her more as a roommate or sister than a spouse. Sometimes when they were making out, he confided, he didn't get a hard-on; he worried that maybe his plumbing wasn't working as well as it used to.

Ryan was not only concerned about his ability to become aroused; he was also questioning Aviva's feelings towards him. He wondered if she still desired him, if she was no longer physically attracted to him. "I want to know that she still wants me," he said. He explained that he felt some urgency about getting this problem "fixed," since he was fifty-six, in the "autumn" of his life, and worried that time and age would soon make it harder to enjoy being sexually active together. (I suggested that making things better might be more realistic than "fixing" things.) He shared that he had sometimes even considered finding sex elsewhere and had openly admitted this to Aviva (sometimes in the form of a threat during a fight). During times when he is more clear-headed, however, he realizes that he doesn't want to sabotage his relationship with the woman he loves and so is okay—for now—with masturbating to relieve his pent-up sexual energy.

Since Ryan had raised the topic of masturbation, I enquired whether or not Aviva masturbated too. I was looking for signs as to whether her libido (which she said headed out the door four years ago and never returned) was really as absent as she believed. I was interested to hear that she used to masturbate and enjoy it, but that she now had no inclination to do so. I asked both about using pornography as a visual aid when masturbating (for her in the past and him currently). They both shared that this has never turned them on. I made a note to myself to cross that off the list of possible ideas for increased arousal. Aviva, at the age of fifty-four and with no sign of a period over the past two years, did not take me by surprise when she said that her libido had changed. She said she had spoken to her doctor about hormone replacement therapy but that he wasn't keen on this because of a history of breast cancer in her family.

According to Aviva, the onset of menopause about four years earlier seemed to be a marker for the change in their sex life, but Ryan gently reminded her and informed me that of all the issues in their lengthy relationship, sex—or the lack thereof—has always been at the top of their list.

It hadn't always been that way—on this they agreed. When they first met, they couldn't get enough of each other. It didn't matter how tired they were, they'd still be hot and horny for one another and the sex was very satisfying for both. Despite Aviva's self-proclaimed conservative nature, she was adventurous in bed and willing to try different positions and pleasures. Things started to change, they said, around four or five years into their relationship. Ryan wondered if perhaps this had something to do with their inability to conceive. After several months of following meticulously mapped ovulation charts and temperature readings, they began investigating why Aviva was not conceiving. She discovered that her fallopian tubes were blocked and decided to undergo surgery to try to unblock them. Unfortunately, the surgery was not successful and both decided that rather than going the IVF or adoption route, they would let fate decide their future. Neither appeared to have any unresolved resentment towards the other over this decision. Both seemed very much on the same page about deciding to remain childless if "higher powers" intended their lives to be lived this way. Aviva certainly did not think that this period in their lives caused their sex life to change, and both her words and body language made me believe her.

I continued crossing hypotheses off the list as to the cause of their declining sex life. Yes, they understood that a change in sexual appetite and frequency is normal in most relationships. They expected some cooling off from when they were dating and totally into sex with one another, and they knew that living together meant they might take each other for granted and become lazier in the lovemaking department. Still, the normal decline didn't seem to be the entire reason for the change.

Over the course of several follow-up sessions, we continued to explore other reasons why they were no longer having sex or, more specifically, why Aviva was no longer into having sex. I gathered more information about the messages she'd heard growing up. I wanted to know if she felt that sex was dirty or wrong. I wasn't surprised to hear that this wasn't a factor, since I knew that theirs had once been a satisfying sexual relationship and that Aviva had also had positive sexual encounters in long-term relationships prior to Ryan.

I enquired about her body image and found again that although they both recognized changes in their bodies due to aging, neither was inhibited and both were quite comfortable dressing and undressing in front of one another. So, that too was crossed off my list.

Many couples I have seen in my practice have either used kids as an excuse not to engage in sex or have legitimately noticed a decline in the frequency of sexual encounters because of child-rearing responsibilities, but this was not a factor for Aviva and Ryan. In fact, I commented on how not having children made the changes in their sexual relationship stand out even more. They didn't have children to hide behind, nor could they rely on the excuse of being tired as a result of a long day with the kids. They had to face each other head-on.

As it turned out, facing each other head-on was exactly what was needed to finally start making some headway as to why Aviva had lost the desire to have sex with Ryan. It started when I began thinking about Aviva's blocked fallopian tubes and wondering about what else could be blocked. I thought about all the blockages in her body that might be impeding the flow of endorphins and oxytocin.

And so I tried my theory on for size. I began exploring how this couple shared their feelings with one another. They both agreed that Ryan wears his heart on his sleeve and that he is a

passionate man—"good" passionate when he believes in a cause
or is excited about something, and "bad" passionate when he is
angry or upset, and becomes a bit of a "loose cannon." I learned
that Ryan often shouts and says some not very nice things, and
that he is especially poor at validating Aviva's feelings when she
approaches him with a concern. I also learned that Aviva had become an expert at blocking her negative feelings. As a result of
horrible memories related to seeing and hearing her mother and
father engaged in conflict while she was growing up, Aviva vowed
that her relationship would never be like that. As soon as she felt
any conflict creep up between her and Ryan, she would back off
and push the negative emotions down.

When I presented this idea to Aviva and Ryan, they both
agreed that it made a lot of sense. At first Ryan was a little thrown
off. Since their sex life had begun to decline so many years ago,
he worried that Aviva had been burying her emotions that whole
time. I helped them understand that most people living together
piss each other off from time to time and that any negative feelings Aviva held in, towards the beginning of their relationship may
have been related to lesser things. These unexpressed negative
feelings, combined with other contributing factors, such as hormonal changes, had caused their sex life to become less and less
satisfying and frequent. Early in their relationship, Aviva had told
Ryan that she would never turn him away when he approached
her. As a result, he never knew whether she was just "fulfilling her
duties" or whether she really wanted to be with him. After a while,
he began to feel that he was "raping" his wife, and so his preference became to avoid sex rather than feel this way.

Aviva said that she was very good at expressing positive emotions, but that when it came to negative feelings, she kept her-

self pretty closely in check. We explored this in more detail, and I asked her to identify which negative emotions she felt the most strongly. She identified hurt, anger, and resentment. Over the weeks that followed, Aviva reported that there were times when she actually felt that she was slightly more turned on to Ryan than she'd been in a while. She had also become aware, however, that her on switch was very quickly turned off, causing her to retreat. I asked what it was that caused her switch to be so quickly flipped, and it was then that the heart of the issue finally began to reveal itself. It became obvious that when Ryan's self-proclaimed short fuse caused him to react in a manner that sent Aviva into retreat mode, her desire for him ceased. When I asked Aviva if she had a physical reaction to his "hostile" behaviour, she wasn't able to identify any. However, now that I had opened her eyes to the possibility of a bodily reaction, I was sure that she would become more aware in the future. She shared that even when his ranting wasn't directed at her, she still felt the need to retreat so as to avoid any possible conflict. Seeing him swear, throw things, and generally act in an ornery way, for example, when his computer wouldn't cooperate, made her feel that he was creating a hostile, negative environment; it was as if a black cloud was enveloping them.

Ryan described the few times during which his anger towards Aviva got the better of him. He shared how guilty he felt after physically grabbing and holding her. He remembered wanting to shake her. She said that she didn't remember how she felt at the time. I tried to probe deeper by asking her to consider that she might have felt afraid. Perhaps *she* was angry that he was holding and hurting her. Maybe she felt confused about how a man who apparently loved and cared for her, a man she trusted with her life, could all of a sudden become so menacing and threatening. I could tell I was touching on something significant when Aviva's eyes began to fill with tears. I asked if I could probe a little deeper into her emotions, even though I knew that this was one of the most difficult things for her to do—to identify and acknowledge and, especially, to feel.

As I gently probed the dynamics between them and explored how Ryan's tantrums affected her, I became more and more aware of the possibility that it might not feel safe for Aviva to share her feelings so openly in front of Ryan. I didn't want to push her beyond her comfort level. At the end of the session, I made a recommendation. I suggested to Ryan that I refer him to a colleague who helped men in particular deal with their anger, and to Aviva that she either return to me (or to someone else) to begin, one on one, exploring the feelings she had contained for so long.

I could tell that Aviva loved the idea. She didn't say so out loud but I sensed relief from her at the prospect of being able to let her feelings out in a safe environment. Ryan was not so keen. He talked about instead returning together because he wanted Aviva to feel that he was by her side, supporting her every step of the way. He also said that he wasn't going to change after fifty-six years of being the way he was, and he didn't want anyone telling him to contain his anger. I could tell that he was afraid and reassured him that no therapist would tell him to keep his feelings in. I told him that, in fact, he was likely more emotionally healthy than Aviva because he was able to express his emotions (he said that when he vented it was like throwing up after eating something bad, and that he felt much better after), but that it would be a gift to Aviva and to them as a couple if he learned to express his anger in a way that didn't affect her so adversely. Aviva would be giving *him* a gift by learning how to identify her emotions and by receiving guidance on how to share them out loud.

I presented a game plan: each could take some time to work on their own issues and then return as a couple. Ryan suggested that they discuss this proposed plan together and get back to me. Sensing that Ryan might persuade Aviva to continue coming in together, I requested that neither stand in the way of the other getting help. I ended the session by suggesting to Ryan that Aviva would likely desire him much more after he learned how to express his negative emotions differently and after she learned how to share what she was feeling out loud. I felt that the ultimate goal would be to work towards Aviva being able to say to Ryan, "I feel turned on to you again because I feel that you are tuned in to me."

Unfortunately, counselling doesn't always lead to a fairy-tale ending. Ryan and Aviva didn't follow through with my suggestion, deciding instead to take a break from counselling.

A Real Turn-off

Being turned off as a result of your partner's behaviour is very common. Sometimes the behaviour is petty and mean, as we saw with Trevor and Miriam. Sometimes, as with Ryan and Aviva, the behaviour is angry and aggressive, or reminds you of something ugly in your past. Sometimes the behaviour is irritating or annoying. Maybe he blows his nose into his napkin at the dinner table and then drops the napkin onto his plate, or farts when you're under the covers together. You've asked him to stop. He says he will, but then he doesn't. Over time, even a small, non-smelly fart triggers irritation. "You said you would stop and you're not making any effort," you say as you roll over in bed, turning away from him. There seem to be more examples of women feeling irritated by men than vice versa. Is it that men don't get irritated as easily by women's bad habits? Or does the irritation just not turn them off in the same way that it does women?

It's quite possible, as we've seen, for men to continue wanting sex even in the midst of a "bad patch" in a relationship. That's not to say, however, that men are immune to anger, frustration, and hurt feelings.

---

* DAN AND ANGELA *

Dan and Angela have been married for fifteen years and have two children, aged twelve and ten. Their goal in coming to see me was to work through parenting disagreements. I heard from Angela that Dan jumps in when she's disciplining the kids. He says it's because he feels she is too harsh and he wants to protect the children. Unfortunately, his intervention has just the opposite effect: when he butts in, she turns on him instead, and the children end up feeling responsible for their parents' argument. One of their most recent arguments, Dan said, was regarding how closely the children should be monitored when doing their homework. Angela was strongly opposed to continuing to have their computers in an upstairs bedroom. She had seen her older child, in particular, distracted by computer games and Internet chats. In an effort to keep them on track, she had decided to move the entire setup—computer table, chairs,

and computers—to the main floor in order to keep an
eye on them. Even though Dan was opposed to this
idea, saying that the kids were old enough to regulate
themselves, she made the move one weekend when he
was out of the house. When he returned and found that
she had gone ahead with the change despite his opposition to it, he was angry and upset.

———————————————————

Like so many couples who come to see me, Dan and Angela
had plenty of anger and frustration between them. When they
shared the computer situation with me, I enquired as to how the
issue had been previously explored and whether her way of "re-
solving" their opposition was unique to this situation or typical.
Aside from my concern as to their ability to work through issues,
other concerns evolved from my interest to understand how their
relationship worked and to help them think outside the box. After
further discussion, it became apparent that Angela's desire to re-
structure part of her home environment was as much about Dan
as it was about the kids: she was looking for a way to disrupt his
nightly ritual of escaping into the world of erotica and pornography on the upstairs computer. Once the children were in bed, Dan
would retreat into the "computer room," lock the door behind
him, and explore Internet sites that allowed him to release his
pent-up sexual energy through masturbation, he said. Although
Angela said that this behaviour was not upsetting for her and that
she didn't mind, her actions conveyed a different message. She
suggested that it might be nice for Dan to be on his computer in
the living room while she was on hers so that they could spend
more time in each other's company at night.

I explored other reasons why Dan felt the need to engage in his behaviour behind closed doors. He shared that their lack of intimacy was definitely a major contributor and said that he would prefer to be with Angela than be a voyeur of others' sexual acts. He shared his frustration at feeling rejected by her for so many years. "Even when I put my hand between her legs in bed to try and stimulate her," he said, "she normally pushes my hand away or squeezes her thighs together to keep my hand out." She responded with, "Well, shoving your hand between my legs is more like 'let's fuck' than 'let me show you how much I love you.' When you reprimand me in front of the kids and then want to fuck me at night, I feel like nothing more than a vessel for your satisfaction. You can't just attack me. You need to romance me."

—

Angela and Dan, Aviva and Ryan, Miriam and Trevor are clearly different couples with different issues, yet they share a great deal in common, and we can take away some important knowledge from exploring their struggles. When a partner's bad behaviour has flipped your sexual switch into the "off" position, you may consciously or unconsciously use sex (or the lack thereof) as a silent weapon. The bad behaviour itself can come in myriad forms: an inability to disconnect from work, a lack of respect when it comes to your thoughts and feelings, yelling at your children, irresponsible handling of money, forgetfulness, lack of initiative, emotional passivity, or just off-putting habits. The behaviour itself is almost secondary to the feelings it generates: not only does a woman's sexual desire plummet when she finds her spouse's behaviour a turn-off, so too does her respect for him and desire to open herself up.

Is This You?

Is anger taking up too much space in your bedroom? Are resentment and frustration turning your switches to "off"? Consider the following statements and check off the ones that describe you:

- I often don't want to be in the same room as my spouse.
- I look forward to when he/she goes away on business trips so that I can be alone.
- No matter how many times we talk about a problem, it keeps repeating itself.
- I don't feel like we are in sync or on the same team.
- It often feels as if my partner is going against me just for the sake of it.

Did you check off three or more of the statements? If so, it's likely that you are walking around with feelings such as anger, resentment, and frustration, and that these feelings are affecting your desire to be physically intimate with your spouse.

First Steps to Critical Thinking

This exercise is *critical* in two senses of the word: first, it is *critical* with regard to *evaluating* one's partner and his or her behaviour; second, and perhaps more important, it is an *essential* way to ensure that both partners think about and learn how to change their behaviour.

Put-downs and criticisms can take a huge toll on relationships and the degree of connectedness between partners. And yet, it's so very easy to criticize a lot of what our partner says and does—anything from the way he slurps his soup to the way she stacks the draining board by the sink. If you're feeling guilty about this and want to change, or if you find that your partner is pulling away as a result of the way you speak to him or her, this exercise can help. Although you will not be able to complete this exercise at one sitting, you can at least begin the discussion and set up the sheets at home or on a coffee date outside of your home.

On two (one for each of you) 8.5 x 11-inch sheets of unlined paper, turned horizontally, create three columns. At the top of the first column write *My Critical Thought*, at the top of the second column, write *Perceived Criticism*, and at the top of the third column write *I Take It Back*. Keep your sheets separate, but make sure they are easily accessible so that you don't forget what you want to record. If you can't record a thought at the time you're thinking it, consider creating a reminder on your cellphone or tablet, for example.

Each time you have a critical thought about your spouse, write it down under the first column and include the date and time. For example, you may be in the kitchen cooking and notice that the garbage pail is overflowing. Your thought might be, *He never takes initiative to take out the garbage (Jan. 2, 6:10 p.m.)*, The idea behind this part of the exercise is to recognize what you are thinking and then, instead of yelling about it, to zip your lips and write it down instead. (Yes, I know that the garbage will remain overflowing, but does your yelling typically lead to a different result anyway?)

The second column comes into play when you are at the receiving end of a perceived criticism. Let's say, for example, that your husband yells from the laundry room, "I never have enough shirts to wear." You would likely feel that he is being critical about the speed at which you are keeping up with laundry. Instead of responding as you normally might, write the incident down and include the date and time: *Felt criticized about keeping up with laun-*

dry—he says not enough shirts to wear (Jan. 5, 8:25 a.m.). The point of this part of the exercise is to help you become more aware of when you feel you are being criticized or undermined. However, instead of retaliating and saying something vengeful, perhaps escalating the situation, you write it down instead. You will have time to express your feelings later, when calmer heads prevail.

The last column is where you can recognize what you said and indicate your desire to take it back. For example, after your spouse yelled about not having enough shirts to wear, he may have realized that he should have written these words down in his *Critical Thought* column rather than express them out loud—but the words escaped his lips before he could stop them. His recognition that you may have perceived this as a criticism will go a long way towards the development of responsibility and empathy—becoming aware of what the person on the receiving end of one's words may be feeling. Realizing that you have most likely recorded this incident in your *Perceived Criticism* column, he can vindicate himself by recording what he said under his own *I Take It Back* column: *Said not enough shirts (Jan. 5, 8:30 a.m.).*

At the end of each week, when you and your spouse get together to share what you have recorded on your sheets, look for the following:

Under the first column:

- How often did each of you think critical thoughts regarding one another?
- Is there a pattern? For example, are most of the thoughts related to kids or housework? Is there a specific time of day when these thoughts occurred? (For example, only when you are at home? When you are tired?)

Under the second column:

- Share what you felt criticized about.

- Explore why your spouse may not have considered these to be criticisms (that is, why didn't he or she write the thought down in the first column instead of saying it out loud?).

- Ask if your spouse is more able to see them as criticisms now that you have provided feedback.

Compare each other's sheets with columns two and three in mind. For example, when your spouse was looking for shirts and yelled that he didn't have any, he did not initially recognize this as a critical thought, hence its absence from column one. However, once he said it out loud and recognized that you might feel blamed (since in your house it is your job to do the laundry), he might have regretted his words. Realizing that you most likely would have recorded it under your column two, he then recorded it in column three. He should get some "brownie points" for this awareness of being critical, even if it was a little late. In addition, if you wrote down the perceived criticism at 8:25 a.m., and he recorded it in the "take it back" column at 8:30 a.m., might he score even more points for recognizing it so quickly?

Recognizing the behaviours that turn each other off and working on ways to change them, becoming more self-aware so that you can stop to think before you talk (or yell), developing increased sensitivity towards one another, and taking responsibility and apologizing for what you have said wrong (so long as column three gets shorter as you continue this exercise over a period of a few weeks) will help you feel more in tune over time. A word of caution: just because you are ready to put your anger aside and move on doesn't mean your partner is too. Let your partner know where you are in the process and ask that he or she let you know when they are ready to move on too.

If you are feeling good about this exercise and the progress it is helping you make, you can consider extending it by discussing, and even recording, how often you receive *positive* feedback from one another. For example, when he says, "Thanks for shovelling snow off the driveway. I noticed as soon as I drove up to the house," how does this make you feel? Are you more inclined to want to shovel again? Over time, you will likely see that positive feedback is just as powerful a turn-on as negative comments are a turn-off.

Eight

Left Cold

BOREDOM IN THE bedroom is one of the more common complaints couples talk to me about— and that's a good thing! If you're *not* talking about the boredom, then chances are good that you're hoarding a whole bunch of negative emotions inside. And if you're not brainstorming ways to create more excitement and to banish boredom, then your relationship is more vulnerable and open to the possibility of being penetrated by others, literally and figuratively.

It's absolutely normal if you find yourself tired of the same old, same old: same old position, same old bed, maybe even the same wall colour over the years. Boredom, or ennui, may be experienced for different reasons. Your partner's approach may have become too predictable, as may his way of touching your body in the hopes of turning you on. What might have felt good at the beginning of your relationship may no longer work. Or perhaps the boredom is simply the result of your relationship's stage of development. Relations in the bedroom and elsewhere can be quite different after two years, for example, than after twenty-two. Interestingly, boredom can also be more about you than about your partner, or even the number of years you've been together. Are you a person who needs constant excitement and newness? On its own this is not a problem, but it may become one, depending on whom you've chosen as a mate. Maybe you knew from the start that you liked to live more "on the edge" than he does, but you thought that he'd grow to enjoy the activities or pace that you set. Years in, however, perhaps you are realizing that this hasn't happened, and wondering if you will grow even more bored as time marches on. Or maybe the fun-loving person you dated for many years before you married has changed. She's become consumed with her work or with the kids and you feel disappointed that your passionate partner has let you down. Then there's the "normal" humdrum co-existence that often emerges as you go from one week to the next, carrying out the same activities, calling out a few last-minute instructions as you pass each other in the hallway before going your separate ways.

Let's explore how these various types of boredom can play out in a marriage.

Time Changes All

Given time, almost anything can become a bit boring. People who have been in the same job for decades sometimes find themselves wanting a change. And chances are good that the television series you've been watching for years isn't quite as good now as it was at the start; the characters may seem a bit tired, the plots predictable. Is it any wonder, then, that marriage and intimacy are subject to the same changes?

What may be surprising is how quickly boredom can set in. Even a year into marriage—and casting all other factors aside—the chemistry between you will not be as explosive as when you first met. The novelty of newness has worn off, and some things will have become routine. Maybe you don't even like it when he says "I love you" at the end of every phone conversation; it was nice at first, but now it's just a salutation like "goodbye." And though you thought it was nice and neat that he went upstairs to change into his jeans and T-shirt as soon as he walked through the door in the evening, now you're wishing that he would change things up a bit.

✳ BORING OR COMFORTING? ✳

Before you get too down in the dumps about all the routines you and your spouse have settled into, it's worth remembering that there is a positive way to look at the situation. Although you may view your spouse's behaviour as just the same old everyday stuff, there's also something reliable and predictable about it. You know where you stand and you can time what you need to do around it. For some, familiarity breeds contempt; for others, it's comfortable and comforting. It's all in the way you perceive and frame it.

Some couples—especially those who have been married for a while—don't realize how mundane their lives have become until they are less distracted. Many couples have their first child around the same time that the excitement of their relationship is naturally wearing off; as a result, they may not notice it at first. Raising children turns the spotlight away from you as a couple and you move into another stage of your lives together—the busy, hectic, distracted years when you are focused on being parents. (Interestingly, this is also when many men have their first affair.)

But, like all other relationship stages, this too shall pass. As the kids grow older and begin to prefer the company of their friends to that of their family, you will find yourselves once again hanging out with each other. Absent the frenetic pace to which you've become accustomed—when trying to keep up with the kids' schedules and living vicariously through their relationships—you may feel at a loss. If you haven't kept in touch with your partner, the empty-nest years, and those leading up to that stage in your lives, may seem quite dull. Without the kids, the house can seem empty and lifeless. There's plenty of time to spend with each other, but you may find that you'd rather not. The person across the table from you at dinner may seem like a stranger. You may struggle to find things to talk about. You feel disconnected and out of sync. And these feelings will undoubtedly carry over into the bedroom, where sex may be a distant memory, and desire a thing of the past. But it's not too late: this may be the perfect time to have fun and reconnect, to get to know one another all over again and to enjoy the freedom of less responsibility.

For any couple, regardless of life or relationship stage, even positive transitions can present challenges. Perhaps one of you enjoys change more than the other. He may be content to meet up with the same friends every weekend, but you may want to switch it up from week to week. You may wish to vacation at the same resort every year, while he's tired of the same destination and activities. When one spouse wants to change things up regularly and the other wants consistency, routine, and predictability, this can pose a problem for the couple. You may find yourself in a position where one partner cherishes the history that you share and the rituals you have created, while the other has become more and more miserable as a result of the sameness.

Craving Excitement

Not surprisingly, your compatibility outside the bedroom in regard to sameness and routine may spill over into your sex life. Here again, one of you may prefer to spice things up, try different positions, and take workshops to learn how to pleasure each other better. The other may be perfectly happy with what you have. When this disparity occurs, the results can be upsetting for both partners.

✳ ROSE AND FRANK ✳

Rose, a fifty-year-old divorced woman, has two grown children. For the past six years she has been living with fifty-two-year-old Frank. Frank has a teenage daughter of his own, who lives with his ex wife. For the most part, Rose and Frank live their lives without taking their kids into consideration. Rose is self-employed and has a successful career. Frank works for the government, makes an okay living, and clocks out at 4:30 p.m. every day. When they travel to exotic places (at Rose's insistence; Frank would be just as happy to go somewhere cheap and cheerful) and eat at expensive restaurants, Rose grudgingly foots the bill. She requested an appointment on her own because she felt that she had some personal issues to work through.

She entered my office with an air of self-confidence, impeccably groomed and with the smell of expensive perfume wafting around her. She shared that she had found work at a young age and, with her competitive drive and determination, had created a successful business on her own. A self-made millionaire, money was no object and she was used to treating herself to material things that satisfied her expensive tastes. Over the course of a few sessions, Rose acknowledged her tendency towards boredom—not just in the bedroom but in all aspects of life. If she weren't constantly setting new goals at work, she would become bored. If she weren't planning her next vacation, she'd feel she had nothing to look forward to.

It was difficult, she said, to meet a man who could keep up with her—at work or play. Her expectations for her mate were high and she acknowledged this too. However, she firmly believed that since she had worked hard to get where she was, she shouldn't have to settle in love or any other part of her life. Her first marriage had ended because her husband couldn't keep up. She said that he found her lifestyle too frenetic. He was content to spend more time at home but she wanted to be on the move. Ultimately, she had a one-night sexual encounter with a business executive she met at a conference. She found him ambitious and strongly opinionated and this was intoxicating for her. It was at this point that she ended her eighteen-year marriage—not because of the executive but because she wanted something more than her husband could offer.

Six years later, and now well into a relationship with Frank, Rose was ready to tackle her boredom issues. We explored her expectations—both of a partner and of relationships—and the pattern that was presenting itself again. I acknowledged her thirst for adventure, stimulation, and excitement, but encouraged her to explore ways to feel more satisfied with living in the present.

Over time, Rose took more personal responsibility for being bored. She realized that if she wanted to remain in her relationship with Frank (which she did), she was going to have to change her expectations, compromise, and learn how to assimilate their lifestyles. This took dedication and hard work on her part. Through intensive counselling, she was able to reflect on why she was perpetually driven to succeed (her parents' expectations played into this), what alternative ways to live her life looked like, and the skills needed to compromise with her partner. Ultimately, she gave herself permission to "let go" some of the time so as to align her actions and thoughts with her long-term goal—living happily with Frank.

Differing Needs

While it's not unusual for one partner to feel more or less content than the other, some people do not see the boredom as a reflection of something inside themselves, as Rose ultimately did. Instead, some may blame their boredom on incompatibility or different needs within their relationship.

✷ BONNIE AND NICK ✷

When I met Nick and Bonnie, they had been married for eleven years and had three children under the age of ten. Bonnie had met Nick while working at a restaurant. She was waitressing and he was her manager. At the time she was just nineteen and he was twenty-three. She felt good around him and respected by him, and was honoured that he paid special attention to her, gave her extra shifts, and even drove her home when she was working late. Eventually, they began spending time with one another after their shifts were over. He was kind, caring, and considerate—everything she thought she was looking for in a boyfriend. After losing her virginity to Nick, however, Bonnie's feelings began to change. Nick's kind, considerate ways became too predictable. She was envious of her friends, who were out partying with different people. She didn't feel ready to settle down. Around this time, however, Bonnie discovered that she was pregnant. Nick proposed and she accepted, knowing full well that she would not have said yes had she not been pregnant.

They married three months before their child was born, and life was as Bonnie had predicted it would be: stable but boring. The one bright spot was being a mother. Bonnie wanted another child, so she became pregnant again and settled into raising her two children—and then a third—while Nick continued to manage the restaurant where they'd first met. It was at a parent-and-tot morning that Bonnie met Grace. Grace was also a stay-at-home mom, and also bored in her relationship. As their friendship grew, so did their desire to look for excitement away from home. They began going on Internet chat sites "for fun," though Bonnie admits to having "cheating on my mind."

Sometimes, a relationship seems doomed from the start. At a one-on-one session, when Bonnie told me, "I feel that ours is more of a platonic friendship but I don't want him as my lover," I realized that even with help or suggestions for change, her mind was likely made up. She didn't want him as her lover and there was minimal or no motivation to explore or try out ways to make things different between them.

Bonnie was grateful to have created three beautiful children with Nick and felt that she couldn't have asked for a more dependable, supportive father for them. However, she regretted the way her life had turned out and couldn't seem to get past the fact that her needs differed from his. I wasn't surprised when they eventually parted ways, after she was caught having a relationship with someone she met online. Last I heard, Nick was dating someone else and Bonnie had moved in with Peter, the man with whom she'd had the affair.

Had Bonnie not been pregnant, she would likely not have married Nick, who even before marriage had become boring and too predictable in her eyes. She craved more than she believed he was able to provide and she felt that there was an incompatibility that loomed large even before she said "I do."

When Both Become Bored

For Rose and Bonnie, the boredom in their relationship was one-sided; they both craved something more while their spouses seemed content with the status quo. In those cases, it's often best for the partner who is experiencing the boredom to seek individual counselling first. However, when boredom is experienced or expressed by both partners, couples counselling may be more productive.

Typically, it is the woman who asks her husband to go to counselling with her, and she is also typically the one who calls to schedule the appointment. Some husbands come more willingly than others; some are there because they have been given an ultimatum. Even though the latter is not ideal, the resistance is often temporary. Once the husband realizes that I am not biased towards his wife, nor there to judge them, he usually shares more than either had anticipated. Desire (even if subconscious) for variety in life in general is often equal for both genders. However, when it comes to being bored with sex, it appears that men have a slightly different take on the situation: so long as men are "getting it," so to speak, they don't seem to be as concerned as women about changing positions or environments to keep their juices flowing.

Having said this, I've yet to meet a man who will refuse his wife's suggestions to change things up. So, if she wants to wear a maid's outfit with crotchless underwear, he will likely be a very willing role playing partner, and even if it doesn't turn his crank to see other couples having sex (or to have sex with anyone other than his wife), it is unlikely she will have to put a collar around his neck (unless they're exploring S & M) in order to drag him to a swingers club.

A swingers club may seem an extreme way to banish boredom from your sex life, but many couples have chosen it as a lifestyle or even as a place to go for an occasional date night out. The bottom line is that alleviating boredom begins with talking about what it is that is boring you. It's important to determine where the boredom is coming from. Is one or the other of you hoping for something different than what you got? Does one of you constantly crave newness? Or has boredom slowly crept up on both of you over the years? Once the root cause of the boredom is determined, the next step is to talk it out, identifying just what has become mundane and figuring out—together—ways to spice things up again.

* TRISH AND GEORGE *

Trish and George had known each other for two years before they moved in together. When they came to see me, six months into living together, I learned that they both felt they were drifting apart. George shared that what had first attracted him to Trish was that she seemed like "a badass with a good heart." He thought that they would enjoy an exciting life together as "partners in crime," he said, laughing. He worked as a salesman at a motorcycle dealership and she as a tattoo artist by day and a cashier at a movie theatre on weekends.

Their problems began when she took on the job at the theatre. It was a unilateral decision on Trish's part, brought on by her worries about ending up like her parents, who were always short of money. However, Trish's new job took a huge toll on their relationship. With more spare time on his hands over weekends, George got together with friends—drinking and clubbing. Trust had never been an issue between them, but when George started coming home inebriated after Trish's six-to-midnight shift, once with a women's business card in his shirt pocket, she began to doubt him.

She shared her concerns, but George blamed her, saying that her weekend job was driving a wedge between them and that they weren't having fun with one another anymore. Hanging loose, letting his hair down, and shirking responsibility on weekends was what George liked to do—preferably with Trish by his side. Even though they had loved their carefree, spontaneous lifestyle, he felt that for her, it had become all work and no play. He said that their lives had become boring and he was thinking that maybe they should part.

Trish and George came to see me at just the right time—before their feelings of drifting apart led to any irrevocable changes in their relationship. When George admitted that he was thinking it might be time to say goodbye, it shocked Trish into action. Believing that their relationship was more important than making extra money, Trish offered to quit so they could rekindle their fun-filled life.

It was a relatively simple change, and yet it made a huge difference. George appreciated that she was willing to sacrifice her job for the sake of their relationship. He told her that he wanted to go back to doing things like having spontaneous picnics, and sex in the back of her car. She was on the same page. They talked about taking part in activities that they once enjoyed—paintballing and snow tubing on weekends were a turn-on for both of them. Having fun, playing together, and sharing in spontaneous adventures were what George had been missing, and Trish soon discovered that she'd been missing them too. Once they talked the situation out and took action, their relationship began feeling more positive again. For this couple, there was a fairy-tale ending. Last I heard, they were riding off into the sunset on his motorcycle.

Boring Sex or Bad Sex?

Up to this point in the chapter, we've focused on how boredom in any aspect of a relationship—including in the bedroom—can often lead to a lack of sex and desire. But what happens if sexual *boredom* isn't quite the issue? What happens when the sex is just plain old bad—the kind that leaves one feeling unsatisfied and empty? How does one gain experience in learning how to satisfy someone else sexually when they don't have the same body parts?

If you're a woman, how can you know what it feels like to have one's penis or testicles fondled? If you are a man in a relationship, how do you know what it feels like when the clitoris is being stimulated? Sure, you can gain insight and awareness if you've been intimate with partners who are willing to share what turns them on and what doesn't. But what if you haven't? What if your current partner has very different needs and desires from your last? (And, by the way, just because you've been intimate with many people before marrying, it doesn't mean that you know what you're doing. Maybe no one had the courage or cared enough to correct you.) And what if you were both virgins when you met? Then both of you will be fumbling in the dark.

All of which leads me back to my original question: How does one learn to satisfy one's partner? The answer is not too difficult: ask! The most important way to learn what your partner likes and doesn't like is to ask for direction. The flip side of this coin, of course, is not to be afraid to offer guidance, even if you haven't been asked. In other words, communicating with one another about likes and dislikes before, during, and after sexual or intimate encounters is crucial. He will never know that you find it unpleasant or even irritating to feel the tip of his tongue in your ear if you say nothing. In fact, he may take your silence as proof that you are too enraptured to talk. And if you don't speak up, she may never know that her hands feel like sandpaper as they rub up and down your penis and that you'd really like her to use lube!

When my husband and I attended a couples workshop at Good for Her in Toronto (read more about our "date night" in chapter 12), we took part in an exercise meant to encourage direction and guidance. We were invited to take turns touching and stroking the inside of each other's forearms, while being directed by the other. Over the course of a few minutes, we guided our partners by letting them know about how the pressure with their palm or fingers, for example, felt and, when needed, how it could be adjusted to feel even better. It was an interesting exercise that could easily be transferred to the bedroom. During our discussion afterwards, we talked about how normal it is for a partner not to share their preferences while being intimate, for fear of upsetting the other. However, there is a clear downside in not sharing: a touch or behaviour will continue to annoy you or be unsatisfactory and will make you less inclined to want to be intimate.

Ultimately, if you don't communicate your preferences for where or how you like to be touched, your partner is not entirely at fault for remaining a lousy lover. I say not entirely, because he or she should also work at learning as much about your body as possible. Education, it turns out, is as important as effective communication.

And by education, I don't mean watching pornography that features stars who were (or at least seem to have been!) former circus contortionists. The positions and close-ups you will see on your screen do not usually depict what happens between the average couple. If you're looking for visual aids that really can help (and not just set you up with unrealistic expectations), there are amazing educational videos to watch in the comfort of your home (see the Resources section for some suggestions). When my husband and I visited the 2014 Sexapalooza show in Toronto, we wandered into a seminar room where a video was playing, showing how women can find their G-spot—the erogenous area of the vagina that, when stimulated, can lead to strong sexual arousal, powerful orgasms and possibly even female ejaculation. Projected on the large screen was a naked woman with her legs spread, a vibrator in one hand and the fingers of the other hand positioned on her genitalia. An audience of about thirty watched as she guided us through her journey towards ejaculation. I wondered how much of the audience was watching for the sheer sexual excitement of seeing a woman masturbate and how many were actually there with a true desire to learn. Regardless, knowing that such videos exist and can be watched by couples or women in private (maybe even with a mirror in hand) is a good thing. Without an intimate knowledge of what our own bodies look like (even those parts that are hidden), what feels good to touch, and how to touch in a way that will increase desire and excitement, how can we be effective teachers?

Dr. Betty Dodson, a renowned sexologist and a leading voice for women's sexual pleasure and health for more than thirty years, is also known for her controversial bodysex workshops, where women come together (pardon the pun!) in the nude to talk about sexuality, overcome the too-often-present guilt and shame associated with it, and explore and stimulate their own genitalia (with guidance). She also offers individual and couples sex coaching out of her private practice in New York. Dodson is a vocal advocate of masturbation, and her first book, *Sex for One: The Joy of Selfloving*, sold over a million copies. In 2008, Dodson teamed up with Carlin Ross, another sex educator and author of *How to Make a Girl Come*, to create an educational website, www. dodsonandross.com.

"Masturbation is how we learn to like our genitals, discover our sexual responses, and build sexual self-esteem," they write on the site. "Masturbation is the foundation for all human sexual activity"[1]

The site also features articles and podcasts about hundreds of topics, such as orgasm, anal play, birth control and condoms, and bisexuality. If books are more your speed, there are plenty to choose from. *The Joy of Sex*, written by Alex Comfort and published originally in 1972, is still a classic,[2] and the "sex education" genre has grown by leaps and bounds since then. Consider *How to Make Love to a Man* by Alexandra Penney or *How to Make Love to a Woman* by Michael Morgenstern as good starting places.

✳ TONY AND MARIE ✳

Along with direction and counselling, education is what I offer a lot of people. I was the most recent of four therapists my new clients had seen in as many years. They had been battling to save their marriage after the birth of their child. Although they were still living together, they hadn't had sex in over six weeks. Now in their mid thirties, they were both unwilling to live a life of celibacy. They were also concerned about parting ways and dissolving their family unit. Despite their difficulties, Tony and Marie had lots in common. They enjoyed skiing, loved the theatre, movies, and travel. The major problem in their relationship was a lack of sex. Previous therapists had made lots of suggestions, including assigning certain nights as "at home date nights" (while their parents had their grandchildren sleep over) and taking turns at initiating sex. They tried some of the suggestions, but the changes were short-lived.

As we spoke, I had a strong intuitive sense that Marie wasn't being completely honest with Tony. It was clear that she felt protective towards him and talked about times that she hadn't shared other concerns for fear of hurting his feelings. As we explored this further and she realized that some of what she was not sharing might be hurting them both, she found the courage to vocalize what she had been holding back for many years—even before she became pregnant with their child. "I'm tired of you coming before I'm barely turned on, and then having to masturbate so that I can orgasm too. I've not told you this before, but I don't even think you know when to touch me, what to touch, and how to turn me on."

Tony looked as if he had been slapped across the face. Marie's eyes welled with tears as she noted his response. She knew that she had hurt him by being honest, but if not now, when? She realized also that by continuing to hold back, sex might never be good for her.

"I didn't know you were feeling that way," he said.

"And I don't blame you for not knowing," she responded. "I should have said something sooner but I was afraid to hurt your feelings. But now I realize that there is no way around this. We have to go through this together."

I asked whether Tony might be willing to attend a workshop about pleasuring women. He said he would and Marie was thrilled.

They returned after the workshop and Tony was happy to share what had transpired. Eleven men attended the workshop along with Tony, and he figured he was right in the middle of the age range. Not everyone was married, but the majority were. To start, they were all asked to share what they were hoping to accomplish by attending. Tony said that he was hoping to better understand his wife's sexual needs and to satisfy her more. Most men were on the same page. When I asked if his goals had been realized, he said, "Absolutely." Marie nodded her head and chuckled in affirmation.

Tony found it especially helpful when the instructor showed them a larger-than-life 3-D cloth model of the female genitalia. She was able to move parts aside to reveal the clitoris as she offered them a detailed anatomical lesson and suggested various ways to manipulate the parts that are most sensitive to touch and stimulation.

Aside from being a lot wiser about what to touch and what not to touch with his fingers and his tongue, Tony also walked away feeling invigorated and inspired to change things up from time to time. He felt more tuned in to Marie's needs and what might work best in sexual positioning and had learned about which accessories might heighten their sexual experience.

Marie reached over to touch his hand and thanked him for showing his devotion to her and their relationship by being so willing to learn more about how to turn her on. She said that not only had his technique already improved, but that he had clearly taken to heart the need to ask her what worked and what didn't. In return, she showed her appreciation by asking Tony to comment on her approach and to make suggestions about what worked best for him.

Last I heard they had attended other workshops, together and apart.

Carlyle Jansen, owner of Toronto's Good for Her (and the facilitator of the group that Tony attended), says that being part of a group experience helps to normalize peoples' struggles. It's not unusual, she says, for people to end up in tears. "For years they've been talking to their therapist or best friend about their unsatisfying sex life," she says, and some women "feel that they are the only person in the world who hasn't had an orgasm." When they hear the same concerns from others, they feel a huge sense of relief that they're not alone.

Over the years, Carlyle has seen a shift in both her clientele and their needs. Women are much more empowered and knowledgeable, and more confident about saying "I don't want to settle anymore. I don't want to have a mediocre sex life. I'm tired of not having an orgasm. How can I have an orgasm?"

Mercedes Jones, owner of the Dick and Jane Romance Boutique in Richmond Hill, Ontario, and host of the popular television show *Bringing Sexy Back*, agrees that women are taking more ownership and are more comfortable with their sexuality than ever before. She has also noticed a huge explosion of women who have been married for twenty-five to thirty years who are no longer tolerating what their mothers might have put up with. After trying to work things out with their partners, some of these women are opting to leave their marriage rather than remain unsatisfied. Many of the store's "at home" parties are actually divorce parties where divorced women can have a good time together while learning about the latest and greatest in sex toys.

Mercedes says that her store caters to an older demographic— mostly married boomer women between the ages of forty-five and seventy, but also in their seventies and early eighties. And while it's mostly women who come to browse and buy, hers is really a place for couples to visit. Aside from sex toys, lingerie, and videos, for example, their location also offers many sexuality workshops for couples (and singles), such as Kink 101 and How to Strip for Your Lover.

It appears that there are lots of ways to add sizzle and spice to a boring or dissatisfying sex life; you just have to be willing to do the work!

Is This You?

Are you left cold by the atmosphere in your bedroom? Feeling uninspired, bored, or disappointed by what barely passes for intimacy in your relationship? Consider the following statements, and check off those that describe you:

- We don't kiss each other hello or goodbye when we leave the house.
- I'd rather watch television in bed than be intimate with my spouse.
- When we're having sex I close my eyes and fantasize that I'm with someone else.
- Sex is one of our rituals—the same night every week, same position every time. Same old. Same cold.
- I'd rather masturbate than have sex with my spouse.

If you've checked off three or more of these statements, it's likely that you're feeling as though your sexual relationship has grown cold, or even frosted over completely. Fortunately, there are many ways to change things up—including lots of small things that may make a big difference. For starters, consider these ideas:

- If you're used to having sex only after dark, change things up by having sex in the morning. You may even find that you enjoy it more when you're well rested.
- Have sex in places you typically wouldn't. In *Toronto Life* magazine's February 2013 Sex Issue, respondents to a sex poll revealed some of the weirdest places they had ever had sex. These included on a bed in the bedding department at a local store and about twelve feet up in a tree (at ages fifty-

three and sixty-four!). Having sex in strange places isn't for everyone, but even making out in less typical spots may lead to better sex once you get back home.

Carlyle Jansen suggests setting limits and parameters as a way of spicing things up. For example:

- Agree to touch, but also agree that no one is going to orgasm for at least half an hour.
- Agree to have sex while kissing the whole time.
- Agree to have sex while touching your own genitals.
- Agree to have sex but only to use your left (or opposite) hands when touching one another.
- Agree to have sex, but face a different way on the bed than you usually do.

First Steps to What I Need From You

Whether the sex you and your partner are having is just plain old boring or downright bad, communication is the first important step in getting things back on track. Since neither you nor your spouse is a mind reader (or at least the majority of you aren't), it's vital that you find a way of communicating your needs both inside and out of the bedroom.

For this exercise, you will need two pieces of paper, one for each of you. Turn your paper so that it is in a horizontal position and at the top write "What I need from you is . . ." Then draw a line down the middle, dividing the sheet into two columns. In the left-hand column, list the numbers 1 through 5. Then finish the sentence "What I need from you is . . ." next to each number. So, for example, you might write:

1. for you not to intervene when I am disciplining the kids.

2. for you to take more notice and comment when I have a haircut or am wearing a new shirt.

3. for you not to push yourself on me after I have said I'm not in the mood for having sex.

4. for you to join me at my parents home every Sunday for lunch.

5. for you to put all electronics away between 6 and 9 p.m.

After you've completed your list, exchange sheets of paper with one another. The column on the right-hand side of the page is the space for your partner to respond to your needs (and you to his). So, he or she might write something like:

1. I can do this so long as you don't call them names. When you do, I feel the need to intervene so that I can protect them.

2. I can certainly do this.

3. I can do this so long as we can find ways to have sex more often.

4. I can't do this but I am okay with going every second week or for you to take the kids and go alone.

5. I can do this unless there is something urgent I need to take care of. If this happens, I will let you know in advance.

Once you and your partner have had a chance to respond to each other's requests, pass the sheets back to the original writer. You may wonder why I am suggesting that you write these requests down and respond to them in writing as opposed to talking them through. It is often easier to respond to a request that is not being tainted by tone of voice. Also, a written exchange can serve as a reminder for each of you at a later date. However, part of this exercise does require verbal communication. This discussion takes place after your partner has had a chance to respond to your needs list. A word of caution: be open to your partner saying yes with certain restrictions, or even saying no with a fair reason. Just because we let our needs be known doesn't mean that what we are requesting will automatically be granted to us. Most times, a compromise can be reached. However, some requests, when turned down, are deal breakers. During the verbal part of this exercise, you may want to thank your partner for responding favourably to certain of your needs and discuss which, if any, are deal breakers for you. You may also be wondering why I have included examples of requests or needs that are not only related to sex. The reason is simple: if one's needs are not met or understood—both in and outside of the bedroom—then the feelings associated with them not being acknowledged or realized can absolutely result in hostile, hurt, or angry feelings towards one another, and this will impact on intimacy and sex.

In addition, any time you communicate successfully, the divide between the two of you will be shortened and knowing that you can communicate with words will lessen the need to use non-verbal cues as a way of expressing unresolved issues or feelings.

Nine

Going Elsewhere

ONE OF ACTOR James Gandolfini's last roles was in *Enough Said,* which was released following his death. In the movie, Gandolfini plays Albert, a divorced dad who meets Eva, portrayed by Julia Louis-Dreyfus. In one scene, Gandolfini reveals that when he was married, his wife never wanted to have sex. But then she had sex with someone else, and he realized that it wasn't that she didn't want to have sex—it was just that she didn't want to have sex with him.

His words ring true, confirming my belief that even within sexless relationships, the majority of individuals (yes, wives too) still feel sexual and still desire sex, but may not be interested in having sex with each other. Even between so-called happily married couples—where there is a lot of love, affection, caring, and companionship—sex is often considered a chore, boring, too predictable, or unsatisfying. When this is the case, both partners may find themselves tempted to stray. In this chapter, we'll take a closer look at infidelity.

In the Beginning

What causes someone to stray? What can lead a previously faithful husband or wife to risk losing everything they've built together over the years? There is no simple answer to explain what leads to an act of infidelity. The reasons are as varied and complex as the men and women who find themselves contemplating or in a relationship outside of their marriage.

Often in my practice, I hear men and women who feel betrayed wonder if the infidelity is their fault, or if they could have prevented it by being less possessive, more sexual, or more open to new things. While an overly possessive spouse is sometimes the reason that a partner gives for straying, it's rarely that simple. Yes, it's true that while a more fulfilling sex life may have caused your partner to think twice, he or she may still have ventured out and flirted with disaster. The reality is that even couples who have a healthy sex life are not immune to infidelity. Even at the best of times, the allure of someone new can be tempting. And at the worst of times, years of not-so-wedded bliss just can't compete with the novelty of something fresh and exciting.

And what about for those in between—those for whom sex is just okay? There's likely no way that your life, filled as it is with domestic responsibilities and financial commitments, can compare to a life where there is nothing much to worry about other than which hotel to spend a few hours in or which restaurant is the most secluded. For some, pursuing sex or sexual activities outside one's relationship is also a way of escaping from reality. Sex with someone new and exciting may be a welcome reprieve from bill payments, arguments about the in-laws, and criticisms about the way you wash the dishes or take care of the kids. All of this, in combination with what researchers have found may be our biological inclination not to be monogamous (more on this later), means you may have to work really hard at fighting the tidal wave of infidelity.

Sometimes a life-changing event brings about an epiphany. Perhaps a good friend dies in his or her prime. Faced with undeniable proof that life is short, you begin to re-evaluate. You decide that a satisfying sexual relationship is important to you, and that you don't want to live in a sexless marriage. Or maybe you lose twenty pounds and, for the first time in a long time, feel inspired to wear sexy lingerie to bed. But when you do, he doesn't even notice, and you're saddened and hurt. You worked hard to lose the weight, and you think you look more appealing, but you second-guess yourself based on his reaction—or lack thereof.

Perhaps you're at a party and meet someone who stirs something in you that has been neglected for too long. Something about the way that he looks right into your eyes when you're talking and touches your arm when he's trying to emphasize a point makes you feel giddy and alive. You're elated by the idea that you may be attractive after all. In addition, your body's reaction to being aroused is evident and undeniable. You may be surprised by your response, especially if you haven't felt this way in a very long time (you might even have thought that your ability to be aroused had diminished to the point of no return). You may distance yourself from the attractive stranger, realizing what more interaction might lead to. Or you may not.

Sometimes the eye-opening moment comes without any help at all. It may hit you one night as you're heading to bed earlier than your partner, eager to pleasure yourself to the point of orgasm. You want to have sex—you want to feel pleasure—you just don't want to experience it with your spouse.

The realization that you are not as asexual as you (and your partner) once thought and are still capable of being turned on, may lead to feelings of sadness and despair. You may find yourself questioning where you relationship has gone wrong, and wishing you could turn back the clock. Or you may feel excited and hopeful about your future. Regardless, the epiphany is likely accompanied by some relief—you now know that even though your libido has been shut down and silenced, it has not gone away.

The question is what to do with this newfound knowledge. You've realized that having more (and better) sex, and more physical contact and intimacy, is important to you. What happens next? The way I see it, you have the choice of either engaging in intimate or sexual relationships outside your marriage (with or without consent) or finding ways to reconnect with your spouse. A surprisingly large number of men and women choose the former over the latter.

About Infidelity

When I use the term *infidelity* in this book, I don't just mean being sexually involved with someone other than the person to whom you are committed. My definition is a wider umbrella, under which you'll find any sexual or intimate act that is performed behind your partner's back. So, if you're flirting or having lunch with a co-worker of the opposite sex and then lying about it at home, this is infidelity. If you're chatting with someone on a porn site, or have set up a profile on a dating site without your partner's knowledge, this is infidelity. If you have reconnected with an old flame on Facebook but are hiding this from your husband, this is infidelity. If you visit a massage parlour (or holistic spa, as they are sometimes called) and finish your session with a "happy ending," or pay for a lap dance at a strip club, this is infidelity. All of these acts—which involve intimate engagement with others—constitute a violation of the implied or explicit rules of your monogamous relationship.

Given that the majority of individuals who are being unfaithful—in whatever form—will not raise their hands to be counted, exact figures about cheating and extramarital affairs are difficult to establish. One website (www.thetruthaboutdeception.com) estimates that about 30 to 60 percent of husbands and wives (in the United States) will cheat on their spouse at some point during the course of their marriage.[1] Many of the arguments on the site are taken from the work of renowned husband-and-wife team David Barash and Judith Lipton. They say that for nearly every species, cheating is the rule—for both sexes. In their book *The Myth of Monogamy*, they write:

> Anthropologist Margaret Mead once suggested that monogamy is the hardest of all human marital arrangements. In attempting to maintain a social and sexual bond consisting exclusively of one man and one woman, aspiring monogamists are going against some of the deepest-seated evolutionary inclinations with which biology has endowed most creatures, *Homo sapiens* included. There is powerful evidence that human beings are not "naturally" monogamous, as well as proof that many animals, once thought to be monogamous, are not. To be sure, human beings *can* be monogamous (and it is another question altogether whether we *should be*), but make no mistake: It is unusual—and difficult.[2]

Noel Biderman, founder of AshleyMadison.com—the world's largest, best-known, and most controversial Internet site for men and women seeking sexual encounters or relationships outside their marriages—agrees. He offers the "not-hard-wired-for-monogamy" argument and says that societal norms have worked to depress our natural condition.

Monogamy, Biderman believes, is a human construct, one that came about because we started owning things and wanted to pass them on to the people who were important to us. The only way to do this, he says, was to create the rule of monogamy. He further suggests that the rule was really created for women, because no man is ever purely monogamous. As proof, he points to brick-and-mortar environments around the world that create socially acceptable venues for male unfaithfulness—strip clubs, massage parlours that do more than massage, and brothels. (Alan Markovitz—owner of strip clubs in Detroit since the 1980s, author of *Topless Prophet: The True Story of America's Most Successful Gentleman's Club Entrepreneur*, and the subject of an HBO/Cinemax reality TV series called *Topless Prophet*—said on one of the shows that strip clubs are "an adult's Disney World.")

The activities that occur in all of these places offer some form of sexual catharsis outside marriage and can therefore derail intimacy within the marriage.

Is it possible that Barash, Lipton, Biderman, and Mead are right, and that monogamy is not working for us? The popularity of pornographic sites, the rise of swingers clubs, and the fact that, according to Biderman, more Americans attend strip clubs than Broadway plays suggest that there may be something to this argument.

Given his line of work, it stands to reason that Biderman believes that not wanting to settle for a life of celibacy is a reasonable excuse for infidelity. His experience indicates that men tend to have their first affair when their wives are pregnant, or shortly after their first child is born. Apparently, says Biderman, they "mistakenly expect their sex lives to be the same as the first two years of their relationship. Now it's been transformed and they adjust really poorly to that. Desire and appetite start winning out and a singular pursuit for sex arises, where matrimonial bonds are no longer honoured."

Interestingly, M. Gary Neuman, marriage counsellor and bestselling author of *The Truth about Cheating: Why Men Stray and What You Can Do To Prevent It*, offers a slightly different perspective. He claims that nearly one in three men will cheat on their wives during marriage, but not necessarily because they are looking for sex. Most, he says, are sensing an emotional disconnect and feeling underappreciated in their marriages. He offers six warning signs of marital infidelity, one of which is infrequent sex (perhaps as a result of the emotional disconnect). "In many struggling marriages at high risk for infidelity, couples have sex only about once every couple of months," he says.[3]

☀ ASHLEY MADISON: THE LIGHTBULB MOMENT ☀

Before founding The Ashley Madison Agency (now simply referred to as AshleyMadison.com), Noel Biderman—now a husband, and dad to two children—was a sports attorney. Dating his future wife at the time, he helped his firm's ex-NBA clients look for secondary careers overseas. He observed that, perhaps as a result of "the stressors of being away from home and family, the pressures of being an ex-NBA player with a lot of expectations or just the general temptation of fandom," that he didn't seem to have a single faithful (to their relationships) client. The lightbulb moment came while reading an interesting article on one of his many plane rides. The writer suggested that over 30 percent of people on so-called single dating sites at the time— 2001—weren't actually single. His mind began racing: Wouldn't these otherwise attached people prefer not to pose as somebody single? What if they could just confess to being in a primary relationship and say that they wanted to pursue something sexual on the side?

And so the idea for a "married dating" or "extramarital" site was born. A site "for people who are not pursuing relationships with consent"—in other words, a site for those looking to be unfaithful.

When Women Cheat

According to Prevention.com, men have been historically more likely than women to cheat (to the tune of twice as often). Today, however, the numbers are approaching even: 23 percent for men and 19 percent for women.[4]

In *Psychology Today*, Robert Weiss muses about the cultural stereotypes that persist when it comes to women and cheating. "Women are profoundly sensual and sexual creatures, just as much as men," he writes. "Yet somehow the idea that a woman in a committed relationship might have physical urges that she wants satisfied elsewhere, especially if her current man isn't quite, shall we say, up for the job, always seems to catch people by surprise."[5] However, Weiss goes on to say that the reasons men and women stray are often quite different, with women more interested in an emotional connection, and men seeking an "objectified sexual experience." He lists ten common reasons for female infidelity, including low self-esteem, lack of intimacy at home, lack of sizzle, loneliness and neglect, and revenge. He also describes a study by Rutgers University's biological anthropologist Helen Fisher, in which 34 percent of the women surveyed claimed to be happily married when they cheated, as compared to 56 percent of the males. As a result, he concludes that "women are more likely than men to have an affair when they're not bonded in their primary relationship (and therefore are seeking that bond elsewhere)."[6]

Biderman too noticed the upward tick in the number of women cheating—and saw a business opportunity. Assuming that male infidelity was a given, Biderman specifically went after the female market when establishing AshleyMadison.com. In his opinion, the mass movement of women into the workplace was a game changer for female infidelity. "They now had interesting people to connect with, they had earning capacity, which meant that should their primary relationship break down, they had the ability to take care of themselves, so inhibitions were lifted." And, he says, other inhibitions were lifted too. "Years ago, when a woman was caught being unfaithful she was seen as an unfit mother and her children could be taken away."

Biderman's bet was that with increased economic freedom, the removal of societal shackles, and the growth of the Internet, "where a woman could find a future lover on AshleyMadison .com or a past lover on Facebook, they were going to choose those paths versus having an affair in the workplace."

The workplace, says Biderman, is where most women began affairs before sites like his emerged. He believes that many women who might have previously considered an affair with a co-worker are grateful for his site. "Women who have worked so hard at school and in their careers aren't going to jeopardize that by sleeping with someone in the office," he says. "When they were lesser in the workplace—maybe in the secretarial pool, for example—they might have been more willing to take that risk. But if they hold an executive position they aren't going to take that risk."

His "secure and anonymous" site, he believes, also removes the risk of having an affair in a woman's "circle of influence." By that he means that if people have the choice, they'd rather not sleep with their best friend's husband because that comes with double the risk. (On this point about risk, Biderman and I agree: in my practice I have seen the tremendous impact of losing a spouse to a friend.)

In his quest to further understand what women want, Biderman did research on his own and looked at other studies too. What Biderman took from one study out of the University of California was that women use the word *passion* when describing what they are looking for.

> [P]assion meaning sex plus something. Sex plus emotion. Attention. Being an object of desire. What women seem to mention more and more on our service is that there was a time in their life when they were made to feel incredibly special—courted, pursued, ultimately proposed to. That's what they're missing. Now they feel like an afterthought. There isn't the communication, they are not being touched or kissed—the things that made them feel good about themselves. An affair almost instantly does that. You can go on AshleyMadison .com tonight, doesn't matter how old you are or how much you weigh, post a photo or not, and you will have half a dozen men interested in meeting with you in three days. And even

if you didn't go through with it, that is a revalidation of some sort of self worth that we all crave.

Whether you agree with him or not, Biderman feels he has helped women. He own field research has shown that women feel alone in wanting to be sexually satisfied. He heard them describe their sexual appetites as "deviant just because they were thirty-five years old and still wanted sex." Biderman says, "It was crazy to me what these women were saying and I felt bad for them." Many of the women with whom he talked said that people viewed them as being desperate, lonely housewives when they cheated. What he saw were strong businesswomen. He wanted to make them feel more positive and empowered.

Even the name Ashley Madison was carefully chosen with a female audience in mind. Ashley and Madison were two of the most popular girl's names in America at the time that the site was established. Biderman felt that if a woman was going to name her child either Ashley or Madison, that meant she would have an affinity for that kind of branding. "And that's what we wanted," he said. "A female focused brand."

We've come a long way, baby.

Sex Addiction

In the section above, I've mentioned some of the common reasons why women cheat, but really, everything you've read in this section of the book could be listed as a "reason for cheating." Feeling neglected, ignored, angry, frustrated, resentful and alone can all lead to decreased intimacy within a marriage, and that decreased intimacy can lead either or both partners to look for something "on the side." But sometimes, the reasons behind infidelity can be a little less straightforward.

───────────────────────────

* BONNIE AND PETER *

In chapter 8, we met Bonnie, who left her husband, Nick, for greener pastures and eventually married the man she met online. Peter was everything Nick wasn't. He was thrill-seeking, adventurous, and very creative in bed. Bonnie wanted to make up for everything she had missed out on since losing her virginity to Nick and was open to being sexually adventurous—both with Peter and, together, with others.

When I spoke to Bonnie, many years after first meeting her with Nick, it had been ten years since she and Peter met online, nine since they married. "Even the scent of him still drives me wild," she told me. Sex was still more than satisfying for both of them, she said, but they had their issues. For example, Bonnie regrets including others in their relationship. "It's caused arguments and jealousy," she shared. "We've never included other men, only women. Peter enjoyed watching us together and I fulfilled my fantasy of being with a woman too, so that was good. The problem was that I had rules for him when he was with another woman, even when I was there too, and he didn't think that was fair." Five years ago, she decided that including others was "fucking up" their relationship and they both agreed to stop. However, since then, Bonnie has caught Peter exploring sexual activities outside their relationship without her. Once, when he unintentionally left his cellphone at home, she called a suspicious number and ended up speaking to a woman from an escort service. Another time, she learned that he had been going to strip clubs on his own, and also found out that he had met up with an ex-girlfriend on a couple of occasions. When she confronted him about this, he blamed "the lifestyle" that they had been leading for his behaviour but said he would stop. The problem is that she's not sure he will.

Bonnie admits that she still has sexual fantasies of her own, but "won't go through with them because of the consequences." She wants reassurance that Peter is on the same wavelength as she and is concerned that without help, Peter won't be able to put aside or control his impulses. She's worried that he won't make a good choice when thinking about what he wants at the moment versus what he wants as his "forever"—her, she hopes. "I explained to him that sex is sex," she tells me. "The end result is the same. You can have an orgasm with me or an orgasm with someone else but if you make the decision to be with someone else, ask yourself: What are the risks and is it worth losing our marriage over?"

Her take on his behaviour is that "it's about his ego, fear of aging, wanting to prove that he's good in bed with someone else. That it's about the excitement and rush." She realizes that he has always been a thrill-seeker "craving adventure and stimulation" and that because he's by nature a risk taker, his behaviour may never change.

As an amateur therapist, Bonnie did well. However, I believe she may have missed something critical in her analysis of Peter's behaviour: many of his actions are also characteristic of someone who's hooked or addicted to the rush of sexual adventure.

Psychologists at the Mayo Clinic "estimate that up to 6 percent of US adults experience some form of addiction to sexual activity, which could translate into as many as ten million people."[7] Although sex addiction has typically been regarded as a male problem, the playing field is levelling out (as it is with infidelity in general), with women often exhibiting a "love" addiction as part of their behaviour.

I suggested that Bonnie and Peter visit the www.sexhelp.com website to complete the Sex Addiction Screening Test (SAST). It provides a profile of responses that help distinguish between addictive and non-addictive behaviour. Depending on the results, they could also pay a small fee to complete another questionnaire, the Sexual Addiction Risk Assessment (SARA), which would provide them with a twenty-three-page personalized report to take with them to a therapist, if needed.

When Bonnie talked to Peter about checking out the sexhelp .com site with her, he refused. He said that there was nothing wrong with him (or their relationship) and that he wasn't interested in any "stupid assessment." So, Bonnie filled out the questionnaire alone, first for herself and then as if she were Peter.

Out of a possible score of between 0 and 20 (6 or higher being indicative of the presence of sex addiction), Bonnie scored a 6; her input for Peter scored him at 9. I recommended that she might want to contact a certified sex addiction therapist (CSAT) (a list of names of trained therapists across North America can be found on sites such as sexhelp.com), even if Peter wasn't interested in getting help.

Fiona Roche, an Ontario-based social worker/psychotherapist, is one such therapist. She studied with the renowned Dr. Patrick Carnes, a pioneer in understanding and treating sex addiction. When I ask her to define sex addiction, she borrows from Carnes's book, *Don't Call It Love*: "It is a pattern of out of control sexual behaviour or fantasy which is repeated without regard of the consequences to yourself or other people. Its primary goal is to medicate or prevent unpleasant feelings." Roche calls it a "disease of intimacy" and says that it falls under the category of a behavioural addiction, like gambling or an eating disorder.

"One of the problems when dealing with addicts is that there is a great deal of denial," she says. Very few come into recovery while addicted unless they have faced some consequence in their life—such as in the workplace or in the marriage; for example, a wife who says that she's not willing to live with him unless he works on changing his behaviour."

In the end, that's what Bonnie did: she told Peter that she needed him to go with her so that they could both get help or she was going to leave the relationship. Unfortunately, unless Peter is personally motivated to change, the indicator for success is not high. Roche says that treatment is a long-term process, sometimes taking years before the sex addict is in full recovery. This is bad news for many addicts who want immediate results. But there's no way around it.

Why Does Sex Addiction Happen?

You may be wondering why Peter felt the need to continue to pursue sexual activities with others, despite being sexually satisfied at home. Although Roche could not comment specifically on Peter and Bonnie, never having met them, she says that having a propensity towards any addictive behaviour—overindulgence in sex, alcohol, or food, for example—is both learned and inherited.

She says that when she interviews an individual who may have a sex addiction, she wants to find out whether the behaviour is "at a healthy level or at a level of misuse or abuse. Has it developed into a pattern of behaviour? Is the behaviour a way of medicating feelings? In the short term, addictions will work to ease the pain as they download the feel-good chemicals in the brain," she says. "Neuroscientists are telling us that this is a brain disorder, just like alcoholism, for example. Any addiction has the power to take control over you. Over time, it reaches a compulsive level and you can see a pattern of behaviour. He or she is in extreme distress about the behaviour, wants to stop but is unable to. They may stop for a few months, but then they creep back into it."

Unlike some other behaviours that are also harmful to intimacy within a marriage—a lack of attention to one's spouse, perhaps, or issues that bring on feelings of anger and frustration—sex addiction must be treated with therapy. This is not a problem that you or your partner will be able to solve on your own.

Our Affair with Technology

In addition to husbands and wives being unfaithful with real people in the real world, these days we also have to cope with the possibility that our spouse is engaging in secretive sexual or intimate behaviour in the virtual world. Given that we live in the twenty-first century, with all of the amazing gizmos and gadgets that the technology revolution has brought, it's worth spending a bit of time considering the impact that this technology might have on a marriage.

Where's My Cell?

A client recently arrived at my office for her 5:30 p.m. appointment. She apologized that she wouldn't be able to pay me at the end of the session, as she usually does, because she had recently misplaced her purse. She said that it wasn't at her office when she left at the end of the day, and that her kids couldn't find it at home. Despite the fact that her wallet and all of her personal information was in the purse, she wasn't as frantic as I might have imagined she'd be. "All I can say is thank goodness I had my phone in my pocket," she said, holding it up. "I would've really panicked if I didn't know where this was."

Most of us have become reliant on our cellphones and obsessive about checking emails, texts, and social media apps, and technology has become the bane of our existence at home. So, it's not just our children whom we nag to get off their computers, put their phones away, or turn off the television at dinnertime—it's our partners too. And in some way, seeing our partner with a screen up against his face or playing the latest crazy mindless game on her iPad agitates us more than seeing our kids doing the same. Why? Because we justify our children's idle play by reminding ourselves that they will have plenty of time to be responsible adults. Our partners, on the other hand, are supposed to be responsible already. They are not supposed to be choosing a word game on their Android over helping the children with homework or figuring out which hotel to stay in on your upcoming family vacation.

In my practice, I observe that feelings of anger and frustration often surface regarding a partner's use of technology. He might say, "She checks her emails before she's even out of bed in the morning." or she might say, "I can't drag him away from his computer to come to bed at night." Yes, frustration and anger are typical emotions when a spouse is off in his own little world when he's supposed to be an active partner, but so are feelings of disconnectedness, rejection, and loneliness. The partner who has come to see me often feels ignored, or not as important as the activity with which their spouse is involved. And let's not forget the fear of what that activity might be. Technology promotes underground activity. In an age of encryption and password protection, it's harder to keep track of what your partner is up to (unless you download an app to do it for you). Talking of which, I recently became aware of a new app called BroApp. Developed as "your clever relationship wingman," which "automatically messages your girlfriend sweet things so that you can spend more time with the Bros," I've heard that adulterers are now using it too! My advice to couples on this front is simple: each should have unlimited access to the other's technological devices and passwords, when asked. If this is not the case, there is always room for suspicion and distrust and this does not promote a feeling of connection or wanting to be intimate.

* BIGGER IS BETTER? *

It appears that technology in the form of a handheld device—anything from a cellphone to a laptop, for example—can cause a feeling of disconnect between couples. Anything larger—a TV, for example—doesn't have as big as an effect. Maybe the smaller the device, the greater the feeling of distance created between you. When you're watching television, there's lots of opportunity for interaction, like snuggling together, or watching a mutually enjoyed show. A laptop may still create some room for sharing. Looking at or interacting with a smaller device such as a cellphone is typically a solitary activity, turning the device itself into a shield or barrier. When couples don't recognize the incredible impact that this small piece of machinery is having on their relationship, the consequences can be severe.

Human Relationships and Technology

Russell Clayton, a Ph.D. student at the University of Missouri, has examined just how severely relationships are impacted by technology—social media in particular. While observing a counselling session between a psychologist and a couple, he was curious to hear just how prominent a concern Facebook had become in their relationship. The husband complained about how they never talked because his wife was always on Facebook. Furthermore, he was concerned and suspicious that she might have reconnected with her ex on the site. He felt very much in the dark because he didn't understand Facebook's inner workings. This session got Clayton thinking about a potentially negative side to social networking. He invited another student and a professor to join him in creating a study to determine whether Facebook, in particular, is to blame for cheating, breakups, and divorce.

They recruited 205 subjects, with the only criteria being that they were Facebook users. The subjects ranged between 18 and 82 and were 60 percent female.

The users were asked to answer sixteen questions online that measured Facebook-related conflict within their relationships (current or former). One of the questions, for example, was, "In your current or former relationship did you ever experience arguments with your partner because of Facebook use?" The researchers asked how often the users logged onto Facebook (once an hour or more, daily, weekly, or monthly). They also asked about the length of time that the user had been in his or her current or former relationship. They hypothesized that if the user and his or her partner was on Facebook excessively (meaning every hour or more), to the point where it was creating conflict or arguments (which often included jealousy related to reconnecting with ex-partners), this was a predictor for emotional and physical cheating, breakup, and divorce.

Their results, in fact, did support their hypothesis that increased usage of Facebook predicts increased conflict, which, in turn, increases the chance for a negative outcome. However, they found that this was not true for couples who had been in a relationship for more than three years. Clayton suspects that "if you've been married for a long time, Facebook isn't a threat to your relationship." (I'm not so sure. I'm thinking that this may also have to do with the reality that the longer one is married, the more there is to fight about, so Facebook may not stand out as the most prominent cause of conflict in a relationship.)

In an article summarizing the results of their study, Clayton and his fellow researchers write that "Internet use in general, not just SNSs [social networking sites] have been shown to influence romantic relationship quality negatively." They cited another study in which it was found that "compulsive internet users reported greater conflict with their partners, more feelings of exclusion and concealment in addition to lower commitment, lower feelings of passion and intimacy, and less disclosure."[8]

Following this study, Clayton was curious if the same results would be seen among Twitter users. This time, he and his fellow researchers asked 581 Twitter followers the same questions. Once again, they found that their hypothesis was proven true. However, this study indicated that the length of the couple's relationship did not influence the results. In other words, if one is on Twitter excessively, this will lead to Twitter-related conflict regardless of the length that you have been together. It too predicts emotional and physical cheating, breakup, and divorce.[9]

Twitter and Facebook were not designed to do harm to relationships. If anything, they were created as platforms through which people could connect to one another. Unfortunately, sometimes the connection to others takes one away from a primary relationship. Although the studies didn't explore which of the partners—the excessive user or the ignored—cheated or initiated the breakup, my guess is that it could be either one. As a user reconnects with an old flame, for example, a current relationship can be hindered or hurt beyond repair. When a spouse has someone waiting in the wings, so to speak, he or she is less likely to feel motivated to work on a relationship that may have lost some of its sparkle over the years. On the other hand, when the user's partner feels that she is chronically left out or has been replaced by a cellphone, video game or computer, she may be more susceptible to being swept away by someone who gives her more undivided attention. Even though one partner may be more inclined to be on a handheld device than the other, you may see both partners on their cellphones or tablets in one another's company. Often this is a case of "if you can't beat 'em, join 'em." Unfortunately, this is a no-win situation: when both people are perpetually on their devices, there is little or no chance for connection.

Virtual Connections

Up until this point, we've talked about the disconnect that can occur in a marriage when one partner is constantly online. But what about the connection that's occurring at the opposite end of the wireless connection? Is a virtual connection a threat to a real-life marriage? The answer is a resounding *yes*.

A virtual connection with no physical contact can be considered an act of infidelity. Are you or your spouse confiding in someone else online, telling them your innermost thoughts, beliefs, fears and fantasies? Is this not an intimate act? The topic of just how attached we can become to our cyberconnections was recently explored in the movie *Her*. Released in 2013, it's a "science fiction" love story, set in 2025. Theodore (played by Joaquin Phoenix), a lonely about-to-be-divorced businessman, purchases a talking operating system with artificial intelligence. He intentionally sets it up to have a female identity and she names herself "Samantha" (voiced by Scarlett Johansson). Unlike today's operating systems, Samantha is designed to evolve—to learn and grow psychologically. As the movie progresses, we see the evolution of Theodore and Samantha's emotional relationship. He confides in her about his reluctance to let his ex-wife go and Samantha (the other woman) proves herself as a constant, supportive, and involved companion.

As a result of his deepening feelings towards Samantha, Theodore holds back from exploring human relationships, even when the opportunity presents itself. Ultimately, he discloses how he is feeling to his virtual girlfriend and she suggests a human sex surrogate so that they can simulate being physically intimate. This interaction, however, does not work out well and leaves Theodore feeling even more conflicted and confused. Ultimately he learns that Samantha is talking with 8,316 others, 641 of whom she professes to love!

Your partner may not be falling in love with his operating system, but he may indeed be escaping into a virtual world. We often hear that word—*escape*—used to describe our relationship with the online realm, and are also used to hearing that it's sometimes difficult to come back to reality. Not surprisingly, this may threaten many relationships. A partner may wonder what her significant other is escaping from, and to. She may ask: "What's so bad about what we have that you need to escape, and where are you going when you do?"

When someone escapes as a way of coping with stressors, it lessens the possibility of intimacy between the couple. Escaping from reality is a very slippery slope—a journey that needs to be talked about in a relationship. Do both partners want to go there? How can they prevent technology from consuming them as individuals and potentially destroying their relationship?

Cybersex

An online connection that's strictly emotional can be threatening enough to a marriage, so what happens when that connection shifts towards something that simulates the physical closeness of a flesh-and-blood relationship? If online intimacy can constitute an affair, cybersex most certainly does.

According to a poster about the origins of pornography, spotted at Toronto's 2014 Sexapalooza show, 25 percent of Internet sites are porn-related, and 70 percent of the traffic on those sites occurs between 9 a.m. and 5 p.m. on a regular business day.

In addition, many husbands and wives visit sex sites and engage in secretive sexual behaviour right in their own homes, often while their spouse and kids are sleeping. What might begin as a result of curiosity or loneliness can become addictive. So, if you wake at 2 a.m. to visit the bathroom and find your spouse still on his computer, or if he suddenly protects his passwords on his electronic devices, chances are good that he's engaging in something—often sexual—that he doesn't want you to know about.

Fiona Roche says that cybersex addiction (compulsive sexual arousal or activity via the computer/Internet) is one of the fastest-growing sex addictions. "We call it the crack cocaine of sex addiction," she says. "It's highly accessible, affordable, and private if you want it to be." She notes that "repetitively looking at images on the Internet will change the set point for arousal in the brain." In other words, after some time, you will no longer be aroused by certain stimuli, and so will look for more and more extreme images to keep you aroused.

Over the past twenty-five years, as the Internet has grown, so has the proliferation and popularity of pornographic sites. Excessive exposure to pornographic images can have serious effects on a relationship. In *7 Keys to Lifelong Sexual Vitality: The Hippocrates Institute Guide to Sex, Health and Happiness*, Brian and Anna Maria Clement write, "Pornography stimulates the release of dopamine and serotonin, both naturally occurring brain chemicals. With enough exposure to these porn-induced chemical hits, visual imagery can replace sex with another human being as a more satisfying type of sexual encounter, but one that can be just as toxic to relationships as adultery."

Some couples look at porn together as a way of spicing up their relationship; that's fine, as long as both partners are getting something out of it. But there's a huge difference between spicing up one's relationship by looking at porn together and a married individual locking the door behind him so that he can live-chat and masturbate or have cybersex with women on his screen.

In addition to approaching the use of technology with caution, it's important to keep in mind that excessive use of anything can lead to disastrous consequences. When the behaviour becomes addictive, it can be especially difficult to walk away from, even when one is aware of the negative side effects.

When the Truth Comes Out

There's a universal truth about secrets: they are hard to keep. If infidelity is a factor in your marriage—be it the emotional, physical, or cyber variety—chances are good that the truth will eventually come out.

I've seen this play out in my own practice on many occasions. When I ask couples in my office what their goals are, many say that they want to find ways to resolve their issues and stay together. However, even among these couples, I sometimes hear inconsistencies or sense that one of the partners is not being completely honest. Perhaps his behaviour doesn't match his words, or there are gaps in her story as to where she was and with whom.

Often, I am not the only one who picks up on this. After knowing each other for a while, most partners have a strong intuitive sense as to when their spouse is not telling the truth, but out of a desire to believe that he or she is being honest, some instead blame themselves for being suspicious or neurotic rather than dig for more information. This rarely works for long.

I have also worked with many couples who come to me because the infidelity has already been exposed. Maybe a husband or wife has strayed only briefly (with a one-night stand in another city, for example), or maybe the situation is much more extreme—a partner, for example, who has led a double life for years, with a neighbour, no less. When the truth finally comes out—often after a lengthy period of denial—there is deep hurt and betrayal to contend with. Especially if the affair has been lengthy, the person who has been betrayed will spend countless hours reliving their lives over those years. He will recollect events and family times that seemed happy then but are now forever tainted. Regardless of whether the couple is able to work through the indiscretion and move on, or whether they decide things are beyond repair, the relationship—past, present, and future—is forever changed. Hurt and anger and betrayal are now combined with a lack of trust, and that can be the hardest thing of all to overcome. Not surprisingly, approximately 70 percent of marriages end after infidelity has been discovered.[10]

Is This You?

In the sections above, we've talked about some of the warning signs that your spouse may be having an affair. If you feel that infidelity may be an issue within your marriage, I suggest seeking help from a therapist.

In this section, we're going to focus on whether or not technology is a problem in your marriage. Consider the following statements, and check off any that apply to you.

- You feel as if you are constantly competing with a technological gadget for your spouse's attention.
- You and/or your spouse check your cellphone at least four times an hour.

- You spend more time sending each other text messages and emails than you do talking face-to-face.

- Your spouse often stays up after you've gone to bed to spend time on his or her computer.

- Your spouse carries his or her cellphone from room to room.

If you checked off three or more of these statements, it's likely that technology is having a negative impact on your relationship.

First Steps to Technology Etiquette 101

Take technology seriously. It has the power to change your mind and your relationship. Brainstorm options to ensure that you are in control of it rather than the other way around. Some ideas include:

- Promise to make each other the number one priority when you are together.

- If you feel the need to check your cellphone for missed calls, emails, and texts, don't do this mid-conversation. Wait until you are done talking and then ask "permission" to check. In other words, treat your partner as you hopefully would a friend. A simple "Would you mind if I take a minute to check my emails? I'm waiting for a response from someone" goes a long way.

- If an unimportant phone call interrupts your conversation, let the caller know that you will call him or her back, or, better yet, screen the call and don't respond until later. If the call is important, excuse yourself for a few minutes and, again, let your partner know why you are taking the call.

- When you're out together, either put your phones away or change the sound setting to mute and place them face down on the table. This way, you won't be tempted when you see or hear a visual cue that there is a text or email waiting to be read.

- Recognize the allure of sites that may lead to increased temptation or movement away from your relationship, and resist them. If you are afraid of not being able to resist, then consider positioning your computer in a more public space so that there will be less opportunity to visit sites that may lead to distrust between you and your spouse.

- Plan for time away from anything electronic. So, for example, decide as a family to turn off all technology between 6 and 8 p.m. so that you can enjoy dinner together. This will also give you time to take care of other things around the house or to connect with one another.

- Consider establishing a rule whereby no one is "allowed" to have double screens in front of them. For example, when one is watching television, he or she cannot be checking a phone too. And if your partner is playing a game on his cellphone or watching television, for example, you are less likely going to want to cuddle or have sex, even if he reaches out with a loving gesture. Communicate this! Let your spouse know that if you feel that you're the snack during a break in Words with Friends, you're not likely to respond favourably to his advances.

We've reached the end of this important part of this book—the part in which we delve into all of the things that can go wrong in a relationship, all of the things that can lead to an emotional and physical disconnect. If you are still reading, it's likely because you've related well to most, if not all, of the topics we've explored. If you've seen something of yourself in several chapters, don't worry—that's normal. There is typically more than one reason that couples stop having sex with each other. Working through the exercises at the end of each chapter, regardless of whether that particular chapter applies to you, is a worthwhile endeavour. It certainly won't do your relationship any harm, and may do a world of good. In the next section, we'll discuss in greater depth how you and your spouse can get back on track.

Part III

Towards Improvement

Ten

Acknowledging the Problem

A S WE'VE DISCUSSED, half the battle when trying to solve a problem is knowing what, precisely, the problem is. After reading Part II, you should have a much better sense of what's gone wrong in the sex department of your own relationship. The next step, then, is to acknowledge the problem as a couple.

At a very basic level, the problem is fairly straightforward: the magnetic chemistry and flying pheromones are no longer as evident as they were at the beginning of your relationship. If you've been married for a considerable stretch of time—say, more than a decade—you'll already be aware that the delightful "honeymoon" phase is, in fact, the shortest phase in your marriage. Time, domestic responsibilities, aging—all of these combined wreak havoc on your sex life. It's worth remembering, at this stage, that this is normal, and that it's also completely normal to have to work at your relationship—to nurture, grow, and foster the positive feelings between you and your partner, and to look for input from others when you've run out of ideas yourselves.

Dr. Amy Muise, a postdoctoral fellow in the department of

psychology at the University of Toronto, who studies sexuality and romantic relationships and has a special interest in how couples can maintain sexual desire over the course of a long term relationship, says that "When people have realistic expectations and understand that desire for one's partner changes over time, and that a good sexual relationship takes time and effort, the benefits to their sex life and overall relationship are greater than those who believe that long-term sexual desire is easy and effortless."

In this chapter, we'll talk about ways that you and your spouse can define and agree on your particular issues, and we'll explore ways for the two of you to "talk it out" so that you can move towards a more intimate, sexually satisfying relationship.

The Talk

If you know someone who is contemplating marriage, I urge you to share with them that having a frank discussion about their beliefs on sex and monogamy before they get married is as important as talking about whether they're going to share bank accounts, where they'd like to live, whether they're going to have children (and how many), and what religious beliefs, if any, they are going to raise them with.

There's always the risk that this discussion might actually lead to couples not marrying. (Perhaps that would be a good way of reducing the high divorce rate!) Or perhaps the intended might end up defining their union as something other than a monogamous marriage. They might, for example, discuss alternative sexual paths to explore together or apart. The reality of today is that many couples—even young couples who are not experiencing any decline in sexual desire or frequency—are opting to expand their relationships beyond traditional boundaries.

Even though you have most likely been married for a while, don't worry that it's too late. You too can still have an eye-opening discussion about relationship issues you may never have discussed before, define where you are at—both good and bad— and set common goals you want to work towards.

How We Talk About Sex (or Don't)

Before you begin talking about and working towards a common goal, it's important that you define the problem to make sure that you're in agreement. For some couples, this step is the hardest one of all. It's not unusual for women, in particular, to withdraw from or deny sex as a way of communicating much deeper underlying feelings that they are not able (or prefer not) to express in words to their partners. Perhaps she feels that they don't speak the same language (metaphorically speaking), or perhaps she's tried to express her feelings in the past and has failed. If so, she may have arrived at a place where she uses her partner's "language"—sex—to speak volumes. Since men often see sex as a way of communicating love, women can consciously or unconsciously communicate their "loss of love" (or like) by not engaging in it. And in some ways, this action gets the message across loud and clear. Withdrawing from the sexual arena will certainly get a man's attention. The problem is that men may still not get what their wives are upset about. What they *do* get is that she is not interested, which can make them feel unloved, unappreciated, unattended to, rejected, and hurt. None of this leads to positive changes or results.

I have seen a number of negative outcomes when the pursuing partner has had enough of excuses or feeling rejected and simply decides to join his partner in their silent pact of abstinence rather than fight it. One obvious outcome is that one or both partners begin seeking intimacy—often emotional intimacy before sexual—outside the marriage. Another outcome is that the relationship moves from one of lovers to that of platonic friends or roommates. Both of these outcomes have been discussed in greater detail in previous chapters. In most cases, this leaves one or both partners feeling that there is a void or a missing piece in their relationship.

Naming the Problem

Even in relationships where a sexual stalemate has been reached, there is usually a time at which one of the partners becomes frustrated and lets his or her partner know. Unfortunately, this often comes in the form of a volcanic eruption of words after months or years of containing feelings of frustration, rejection, and hurt. This is often the point at which I receive a call for help. When people call me after years of making excuses and tell me how they are feeling, I hear words such as *lack of intimacy, feeling disconnected,* and *not into each other anymore.*

Being able to talk and hear one another, to compromise and learn each other's language—these are essential skills for couples to develop. In order to begin repairing your relationship, you need to talk to each other, to be honest about your feelings and concerns. A good place to start is for each of you to write out and finish the following sentence, and then read it aloud to one another:

"For me, the biggest problem in our relationship right now is _____."

One word of caution before you begin: do not use words such

as *you*, or any other word that places blame or responsibility. So, for example, try to avoid something like:

"For me, the biggest problem in our relationship right now is that *you* want to have sex all the time."

It is better to say: "For me, the biggest problem in our relationship right now is that there seems to be a difference in the amount of sex that each of us wants."

Or

"For me, the biggest problem in our relationship right now is that we're disconnected and haven't had sex in months."

This way, you can identify the problem and place it outside the relationship so that you can each look at it more objectively. By not placing blame, you also leave less room for a defensive reaction, which is likely to shut down communication right away.

If, despite your best intentions at remaining calm and neutral, your partner begins to get angry or upset, try to gently steer the conversation back on track. One of the biggest challenges I see couples face when trying to talk through an issue is that they regularly veer off on tangents that have nothing to do with the initial concern. It's easy to rise to the bait when this happens, but often nothing gets resolved as a result. If you are unsuccessful at bringing your focus back to naming the problem between you or if the conversation gets heated, put things on hold for a couple of hours or even until the following day rather than allowing things to move in a negative direction. If you're not successful after several attempts at trying to work towards identifying the problem, then you may need to work with a therapist who can help facilitate and mediate your discussion. Whether you determine the problem alone or with outside help, you may also want to discuss your next steps, as in whether you might want to attend workshops and seminars or watch self-help instructional videos together.

Talking about Monogamy

Once you and your partner have become more comfortable talking about sex and intimacy within your marriage, it may be a good idea to explore where you both stand on the subject of sexual monogamy. As you move towards repairing your relationship, and perhaps exploring ways to spice things up, this is a necessary conversation to have. If either of you has a secret agenda or beliefs about the way in which you choose to live your life, it will ultimately create a rift between you and your partner.

Other than discussing your beliefs on a general basis, here are some specific yes/no statements each of you can respond to (out loud is best) to help determine whether or not you choose to be sexually monogamous in your relationship with one another and why:

- I want to stay in a monogamous relationship with you because I believe in staying together as a way of supporting and protecting our children.

- I want to stay in a monogamous relationship with you because I support the idea of passing inheritances down to you.

- Although I understand that it is "normal" to want to occasionally be with others, I choose not to step outside of our monogamous relationship for fear of the consequences of doing so. These may include jealousy, a severing of trust, a breakdown in communication, losing some of what I cherish and, of course, divorce.

- I choose to remain in a monogamous relationship with you because I am afraid of how I'll manage the kids' morning routine without you around.

- I choose to remain in a monogamous relationship with you because I'm afraid of losing my house and financial security. (Other related reasons may include wanting to tuck your kids into bed every night or not wanting to start dating all over again.)

- I choose to remain in a monogamous relationship with you because I subscribe to religious beliefs that support monogamy and I don't want to be condemned as a result of being unfaithful.

- I don't want to go against my personal beliefs and commitment to values such as loyalty.

- I recognize that as normal as it is to look at other men (or women), or even to fantasize about others, I don't want to risk losing what we have for the sake of satisfying my sexual desires.

- I choose to remain in a monogamous relationship with you because you are my one and only. You are my soul mate. I don't find anyone else as attractive and wonderful as you are.

- I choose to remain in a monogamous relationship with you because I love and value what we have beyond our loss of sex and intimacy and believe that as a result of our strong foundation, we can work on our problem.

Your spouse's yes or no responses to the above statements will reveal their personal beliefs and their commitment to living a monogamous lifestyle. It helps to go into this exercise with your rose-coloured glasses removed. Try to maintain an open, realistic state of mind. If you do, you are more likely to have an interesting, honest dialogue about the extent to which either of you is willing to work on your relationship. Even if some of the responses are upsetting at first, the upset may lessen as you talk more and appreciate your partner's honesty. However, if your spouse is consumed by fantasies about being with others, and only choosing monogamy for fear of taking care of the kids on his own, this may signal a deeper problem in your relationship—one which may not be as easy to work on without professional help.

I recognize that even if you subscribe to monogamy, your current situation may still be a challenge. Ten or twenty years into a now sexless marriage may have you questioning your choice. Or maybe you still believe in monogamy but don't want to be with the person to whom you made a commitment. The best option is to let your partner know your feelings before you change direction. It takes courage to let your partner know how your feelings have changed, how your desire to be with others has increased, and then to try to work things out—together or apart. If you'd rather stay together, even if your feelings have changed, it's best to try to find a way to bridge your divide, give your partner an opportunity to work with you on turning things around, or to part ways before you engage in another relationship.

The bottom line is that there are almost always red flags (loss of sex and intimacy being two of them) that the relationship is faltering. Rather than waiting and watching its demise, you can take action by communicating with one another. Once you are on the same page, you can work together towards something better.

Eleven

Re-establishing Intimacy

'M HOPING THAT after all you've read so far, you're eager to re-establish intimacy with your spouse. Even if you don't want to jump into having sex just yet, know that reconnecting on an emotional level can move you in the right direction.

There is a lot to be considered as you approach the runway towards intimacy—setting the mood, getting your timing right, and talking, talking, and more talking. In addition to the exercises you've already encountered, this chapter is jam-packed with information to get you started.

Are You in the Mood?

This is probably as basic a piece of advice as you'll ever receive, but it's worth stating: before you start down the road to an intimate encounter, it's important to know what both partners want. It's possible that one or both of you is not in the mood for sex. If that turns out to be the case, you may want to consider what you *are* in the mood for. As we know, sex isn't the necessary destination for every couple, or the end requirement of every intimate encounter. Sometimes, feeling closely connected to one another can result from being together in ways that don't involve having intercourse—tender kissing and holding each other close, for example.

Some couples are more interested in outercourse (no, I didn't make this word up) in the form of non-penetrative sexual activities such as frottage (more commonly known as dry humping, or rubbing up against someone either with clothes on or naked) or mutual masturbation, also known as manual intercourse, where you either stimulate your own genitals manually or ask your spouse to lend you a hand—literally. In other words, not being in the mood for having his penis in your vagina doesn't mean that you're not interested in anything at all. Being able to share your feelings with each other and respecting each other's moods and desires is an especially important part of connecting and understanding one another.

This point is underlined when we consider that one of the reasons women say that they back off when their husbands approach them, even if just to make out, is that they're afraid that if they show interest in kissing even, he might assume it is a prelude to intercourse. Many worry that they will be giving him false hope. So, instead of advancing towards a kiss, she backs off, afraid of giving the wrong impression.

She may be especially careful about not leading him on when they are in a situation that is conducive to having sex—alone at home without the kids, for example, or in bed with the lights out. In these instances, it might make sense for her to suggest the boundary game.

The Boundary Game

Anytime you're not in the mood for intercourse, per se, but are okay with taking part in other forms of intimacy, tell your spouse that you'd like to play the boundary game.

If your partner reaches out for you and you're worried that you aren't going to satisfy his goal, let him know that you'd like to establish a few boundaries—bodily boundaries—for what happens next. You might, for example, let him know that your boundaries are your neck up.

Then ask him if he'd like the same boundaries established on his body. He has the right to say that his body has no boundaries, but it's your choice if you want to touch him below his neck. No pressure.

If he's stumped for ideas on what to do within your boundaries, feel free to make some suggestions. He could kiss and caress your face, stroke your hair, or give you a scalp massage. And you, of course, could do the same for him. The idea is to focus attention on one part of each other's bodies rather than touching all over.

Other times, the boundary can be just your hands and feet, or your chest, or nothing below the belt. Again, the idea is to focus your attention and really get to know one another's bodies and erogenous zones.

Since forbidden fruit is always tempting, your partner may want to venture below the belt, so to speak, even when asked not to. You may need to remind him of your boundary lines or limits.

Before you begin the game, you can decide if it's okay for either one of you to change your mind along the way. After playing for a while, you may decide that you are feeling in the mood for something more, after all. If it's been decided that changing one's mind is okay, then you can let you partner know this when or if you do.

Often, when the pressure to open your entire body up to touch and stimulation is removed, you may be surprised to find that your mood or inclination towards having intercourse changes.

Setting the Mood

Let's assume for a moment that you know that your partner would be up for an intimate evening. One way to ensure a positive outcome and make each other feel special is to work at setting the mood. I am likely addressing the plight of women, in particular, when I write about *needing* to set a mood. Men may appreciate low lights and burning incense, but they're not likely to need them to feel turned on. For women, however—especially for those who have been in sexual "shutdown" for some time—setting the stage, to a greater or lesser degree, can be a necessary step to get their juices flowing.

When setting the mood for a romantic, erotic, sexual, or sensual encounter, all of the senses—touch, taste, smell, sight, and sound—need to be awakened. The "orchestrator" need not provide a symphony of simultaneous sensations, but solid efforts on a few fronts will likely go a long way.

Touch

Know your partner. What does he or she feel is good to touch? Some people like the feel of silk, others crisp linen. If you're not sure what appeals to him or her, ask. And if you're clear on what does or doesn't work for you, don't be afraid to vocalize this. If you're averse to being kissed when he's sporting bristles on his face, for example, let him know that freshly shaven is more appealing to you. He may ask for the same in return (maybe your legs, underarms, or even pubic area).

Consider investing in a portable massage table. This is better than any other surface for at-home massage; it's wide enough that you won't fall off, high enough that neither of you will strain your backs, and maybe even sturdy enough to hold your combined weight if the mood strikes (double-check the specs before you attempt this!). If a new one is too expensive, you might be able to find a secondhand table for sale on the Internet, or from a student at a massage therapy school who wants to sell his so that he can purchase a newer model. They fold away easily and can be set up in a minute or two. Oils (scented or not) can add spice (and lubrication—but be careful about using anything that could be irritating to genitals). Carlyle Jansen, owner of Good for Her, also recommends the use of edible massage bars as a way of building desire. She suggests that the person giving the massage "melt it into the person's back and then move the bar all over the body to relax, seduce and enjoy. Touch the back, then the sides, then graze over the breasts or by the thighs and you will likely find that what happens is a slight bit of arousal that ignites desire. So even if the person wasn't necessarily thinking of sex before, she is now aroused and then you progress a little more and you notice that her breathing is heavy and she turns over on her back and then you're into some sexual activity." Another way to turn up the heat through massage is to allow the act to spark some role-playing. Perhaps you're the naughty masseuse, or your partner is the seductive patient. You never know where the game might take you!

After a massage (if you're too relaxed to give one after receiving one, then trade places on the next at-home date night), relax in a warm bubble bath together. If your tub is too small for both of you to spread out facing one another, try a different position. Have both of you face the same direction towards the faucets, one with his or her back against the wall of the tub (with legs open to accommodate the other person) and the other with his or her back against the chest/stomach of his or her partner. Unless he's behind her, this is not meant to be an entry position towards sex, but more a way to create intimacy and to connect body to body.

Some couples also enjoy using accessories such as feathers to flirt or play with one another. Experiment, and have fun figuring out the things that turn you on!

Taste

Taste is a powerful sensation, and particular flavours have long been associated with heightened sexual desire. And the exploration of this intriguing field is ongoing. In 2008, researchers at the Texas A&M Fruit and Vegetable Improvement Center reported that watermelon has ingredients that deliver Viagra-like effects to the human body's blood vessels and could even help to increase libido.[1] Apricots, black raspberries, figs, dill, lentil sprouts, oysters, avocados, bananas, chocolate, basil, asparagus, and red wine are also considered aphrodisiacs. A dinner featuring some of the enticing foods could get your evening off to a good start.

In the bedroom, some couples enjoy painting the erogenous zones of one another's bodies with specially made chocolate body paint and then licking it off. Others prefer peanut butter or whipped cream. Talk to one another about what tastes turn you on—and off. If you're preparing a dinner at home before licking dessert off one another, you may want to put the garlic and onions away if either of you find the smell of this on the other's breath offensive. (Did you know that in Minnesota, it is illegal for a husband to make love to his wife if his breath smells like garlic, onions, or sardines? She can by law force her husband to brush his teeth.[2]) Although some women or men might find it difficult to tell their spouses that they are turned off by the smell from their mouths (or other parts of their bodies), I'm thinking that if you're close enough to each other to have sex, you should be able to share these types of things. Of course, sharing this information in the least offensive way as possible is highly recommended.

Smell

Some people's olfactory senses are particularly sensitive—in both a positive and negative way. To the scent-sensitive, body odour, scented candles, room freshener, or stale perfume can bring on feelings of repulsion or even trigger a migraine, whereas a favourite cologne (even sprinkled on a pillow) might stir erotic feelings. According to researchers at the Kinsey Institute for Research in Sex, Gender, and Reproduction, "The scent of a man's cologne significantly increases a woman's arousal." Although the researchers caution that a whiff of your husband's cologne won't magically turn you on, they do believe that it "certainly helps put you in the mood."[3]

Know your spouse and the smells that are appealing or displeasing. Certain fragrances are meant to set more of a sensual or sexual mood—musk, for example. And apparently, cinnamon turns some men on. Try to find an incense smell that is good for both of you; once you have, maybe even a hint of this scent will add to the mood of your date.

One of the best books I read while conducting research for this book is *7 Keys to Lifelong Sexual Vitality: The Hippocrates In-*

stitute Guide to Sex, Health and Happiness. Its authors have a lot to say about the power of scent:

- Aromas associated with certain essential oils have been clinically proven to be human mood enhancers, which might be useful during foreplay to stimulate sexual desire and to enhance sexual performance.[4]

- Certain essential oil scents—like lavender, ylang-ylang, and vanilla—heighten sexual feelings.[5]

- Psychologist Rachel Herz, author of *The Scent of Desire*, has made the point that smells we usually think are attractive generally come from people who are most genetically compatible with us.[6]

- Dr. Alan Hirsch, author of *Scentsational Sex* and a researcher at the Smell &Taste Treatment and Research Foundation in Chicago, has shown that certain aromas, such as cinnamon, affect the biochemistry of humans in a way that stimulates desire. Certain combinations of odours create the strongest effects on human sexual arousal; two of the most powerful combinations are lavender and pumpkin, and licorice and pumpkin.[7]

Sight

Other than being turned on by seeing your partner turned on (flushed face, erect nipples or penis, for example), or by seeing the outline of your partner naked or wearing something sexy, there are visually erotic images that couples can view together as a way of arousing sexual desire. For some, just looking at pictures will do the trick, but many prefer moving pornographic images on a DVD or the Internet. Some couples are turned on by watching soft porn, while others prefer something more hard-core—

maybe porn that falls in the fetish or kink category. If one partner finds certain images offensive or repugnant, then these should obviously be reserved for times they are pleasuring themselves alone. If you like the idea of using pornography as a source for increased arousal, find what kind works best for both of you.

In 2006, Carlyle Jansen initiated the Feminist Porn Awards— her response to the fact that a lot of porn doesn't portray positive images of women, people of colour, or people who are larger in size. Carlyle says that "people who are other than the young, petite white woman are fetishized," so she wanted to find and award porn that was more conscious of this. She says that men and women often ask her for porn videos that are more consistent with real life.

Rather than watching sex on a screen, some couples may prefer "private viewings" of their own partners. For women who are feeling adventurous, there are many classes that teach pole dancing, striptease, and belly dancing.

And talking of screens, how about setting the mood by sending a flirtatious invite via text or email to your spouse, inviting him or her to join you for that private viewing or an evening of fun?

Sound

What you hear when you're having sex can be mood-inducing or a mood breaker. For example, if you're having sex and you hear your baby crying, or the sounds of a Disney cartoon in the background, you are unlikely to remain in the mood. The sound of a dripping faucet may make it impossible to focus on your partner. Not convinced? Turn the volume off the next time you are watching a particularly suspenseful thriller on television, or a sappy romance. Without the mood music playing in the background, the images are not nearly as powerful. There are certain soundtracks that are associated with setting the mood for love-making—deep sexy voices like that of Lou Rawls, Barry White, or Donna Summers, or the sultry sounds of a saxophone, can elevate sexual desire. So, select sounds that are sex-inducing for both of you—or make your own!

Timing Is Everything

What happens when you work really hard to set the mood and your evening still falls flat? It can certainly happen. And when it does, one partner can be left feeling disappointed and unappreciated.

✳ KESHA AND SEAN ✳

Sean told me about the time he had planned a romantic at home evening with his wife, Kesha. He had purchased her favourite Belgian chocolates, the wine she most liked to drink and musky-smelling bath balms for their whirlpool tub. He had decided that he would surprise her by running a bath for the two of them, lighting some candles, pouring each a glass of wine, and then feeding her chocolates in the bath.

But when he arrived home from work (late for dinner), he found Kesha in a foul mood. The kids weren't co-operating about doing homework and she was pissed off that he was home later than he'd said he would be.

Faced with his wife's mood, Sean was having a hard time remaining positive about their evening together, but he reassured himself by thinking that a warm romantic bath, chocolates, and wine were exactly what she needed to feel better. He wanted to pamper and take care of her.

After dinner, he went upstairs to unpack what he had purchased for their rendezvous while she stayed in the kitchen putting away leftovers from dinner and supervising homework. Just as she was cleaning the sink and looking forward to a half hour in front of the television, with her feet on the coffee table, Sean came up behind her, put his arms around her waist, and whispered in her ear: "Come upstairs. I have a surprise for you." Kesha wasn't in the mood for surprises but she followed him anyway. When she saw the bathroom lit by candles and the bath filled, she was genuinely surprised but totally caught off guard and absolutely not in the mood for what he had in mind. She didn't want to be a bitch by criticizing his timing or asking how he could possibly think that this was going to happen when the kids were still downstairs (and she was feeling more stressed than sexy), but "You've got to be kidding" came out before she had time to stop the words. She saw the look of utter disappointment on his face and felt a flash of sympathy. At the same time, however, she also marvelled at his inappropriate timing and silently blamed him for not being more sensitive. How could he not realize, she wondered, that she was incapable of switching gears or blocking out the rest of the world just because he wanted her to?

In the aftermath of the incident, Sean shared with me how unlikely he was to consider trying this again. During our session, Kesha apologized for showing a lack of appreciation, and he came to see timing as a crucial part of setting the mood.

Getting one's timing right is as important as setting the mood when it comes to reconnecting with one another. A well-planned and well-timed encounter can lead to a positive connection and a deepening of your desire to be intimate. Dr. Amy Muise, the researcher in the department of psychology at the University of Toronto, says that people's reasons for engaging in sex (within the context of their romantic relationships) tends to be more about enhancing intimacy than about pursuing their own pleasure.

This stands to reason. After all, one doesn't need a partner to be pleasured, or to achieve orgasm. All one needs is a hand and some accessories, if desired. Having sex with another person is about deepening a connection. If there's no affection or respect shown towards one another on any given day (or over all the yes-terdays), then the wedge that is driven between a couple will limit the chances of deeper intimacy. And without the desire for inti-macy, there is no inclination towards having sex—for women, in particular.

Redefining Foreplay

"Foreplay, including touch, fragrance, massage, erotic and emo-tional intimacy, starts the endocrinal engines and helps sex hor-mones to do their work, " writes Dr. George W. Yu in his foreword to 7 *Keys to Lifelong Sexual Vitality: The Hippocrates Institute Guide to Sex, Health and Happiness*. Anecdotal evidence suggests that most of us agree. The results of a sex poll in the February 2013 issue of *Toronto Life* magazine reveal that 91 percent of the 1,305 respondents said that "foreplay is a must." So, if you believe this too, you're not alone. When I asked men and women what comes to mind when they hear the word *foreplay*, here is some of what I heard:

- Kissing and cuddling in bed
- Making out—in bed or someplace else
- Talking face-to-face in bed, often referred to as "pillow talk"
- Stroking, caressing, or touching one another so as to get "in the mood"
- Achieving arousal by touching "private" parts
- Oral sex

I wasn't at all surprised by these responses, as they are typically what most of us associate with foreplay—the period of time preceding intercourse, often as a prelude to sex. But what if we've got that wrong—or what if it's not the whole picture? What if we think of foreplay as a much wider set of events and circumstances?

"Foreplay Begins Yesterday"

When asking people what came to mind when they heard the word *foreplay*, some elaborated. One respondent said, "Foreplay is the whole day's interaction with one another." This reminded me of a conversation I'd had with Carlyle Jansen. "Foreplay begins yesterday," she said. "Yes, it's physical, but it's also spiritual and emotional, and we're going to be much more interested in having sex when other things are working in the relationship as well."

In the absence of tender touching or gentle words—whether

today, yesterday, or the day before that—a couple's desire to connect once the kids are tucked into bed at night is much less likely. And if spouses are actively critical or disrespectful of one another—especially over a period of days, weeks, or months—why would one want to pleasure the other? If this bad behaviour is firmly entrenched, things become trickier still.

If a spouse is mostly argumentative, controlling, or demeaning towards his partner, but then lays on the charm as a way of getting sex, this will most likely be seen as manipulative and responded to accordingly.

I realize that the expectation for both spouses to be on their best behaviour towards one another every day is unrealistic. Everyone has days during which they are more cranky or critical, but if positive exchanges and good days outweigh the bad (I'm thinking by a ratio of at least 80/20), then the cranky spouse will likely be forgiven and given the benefit of the doubt; the good will prevail over the bad and the air can be cleared fairly quickly and easily. Whether it's because you are consciously aware of how negative exchanges are affecting your sex life or not, it's always best practice to talk things through as soon after a conflict as possible. That way, neither partner gets bogged down by negative feelings that block the possibility of opening up to one another so that an intimate exchange can take place.

So long as obstacles are overcome as they present themselves, then the foundation is set from which to create an environment that will foster good feelings and promote the desire for sex. In terms of literally staging the environment, there are many tried-and-true methods that work. Most important, keep in mind that it's not just candles, sexy music, and scent that stimulate one's senses and create a romantic environment. A lot has to do with timing, too.

"What Foreplay? There's No Time!"

Another one of the respondents to my request for thoughts associated with foreplay responded from her ski vacation.

"What foreplay?" she wrote. "There's no time!"

Away from work and household responsibilities (their kids are grown), Kim knew that her husband of thirty years would expect to have sex at least once during their week away from home!

"But we're basically exhausted from a full day of skiing, dinner, and wine and we flop into bed at one a.m. The last thing I'm thinking about is foreplay or sex."

Even so, on the third morning of their vacation, Kim was woken up by an alarm set for fifteen minutes earlier than they needed to get up.

"I looked at the clock when the alarm went off," she wrote, "and immediately knew Paul had set it purposely with a plan in mind."

Knowing that he'd be happy to have sex and looking forward to having it off her plate, potentially for the remainder of their time away, she responded to his cues. "Basically it was get it in and get it out," she said. "I was thinking about wanting to get up, having breakfast, and hitting the slopes. Fifteen minutes was ten more than what we needed."

"So, it was basically 'wham bam thank you ma'am'?" I asked.

"Yes," she responded. "Except there were no thanks."

Thinking back over our dialogue, I realized that Kim did, in fact, have time for foreplay, had she desired it. Ten minutes of time, to be exact. That's two-thirds of the time Paul had allocated to having sex. Since the average time it takes to have intercourse is actually about five minutes,[8] this couple was right on track! But they had done away with foreplay—one of the most important parts of lovemaking and certainly the part that connects couples on a much deeper and more meaningful level.

The fact that Kim chose not to make time for foreplay—instead devoting the additional ten minutes towards getting up and ready for her ski day—is an indicator of several potential areas of concern in her relationship.

- After so many years of marriage, Kim and Paul's relationship seems to have lost its zing. Acknowledging and choosing to spice things up would be an important step towards change.
- Sex might be boring for Kim. If nothing is done to remedy her feeling this way, she may continue to just want to "get it over with" so that she can cater to his needs and hers (that is, needing to get sex out of the way).
- There may be other factors that have affected her desire to be intimate with her spouse—any one of the real reasons explored earlier in this book are possibilities.

In and of itself, intercourse can be a very robotic, mechanical act and does not require any depth of emotion in order to be executed. It's much more difficult to force foreplay. Positive feelings and the desire to connect have to be genuine. In fact, choosing foreplay over intercourse—if you were made to choose only one or the other—would be a healthier choice for your relationship, because foreplay may be a more powerful connector in the long run.

∗ FIERY FOREPLAY ∗

You've no doubt heard or experienced how "hot" make-up sex can be. The level of spiciness likely owes something to the passionate, heated foreplay that precedes the act itself. And I'm not talking about touching and kissing; I'm talking about talking! After (perhaps) days of not talking, there's typically a deep and meaningful discussion that takes place. Sometimes it starts with yelling, but eventually, things calm down. He may say how much he cares about and loves her and how he wants—more than anything else—to be with her. Or maybe she says how sorry she is to have upset him. These kind, caring words and soft gestures lead to the hot sex—a way of consummating their agreement to be kinder and more responsive to one another's needs.

As British Columbia–based psychologist and sex educator Dr. Cheryl Fraser says, when you take away the *e* from *foreplay*, you are left with *for* and *play*—and that's what it's all about. An incredibly simple yet effective way one couple found to have fun while playing and getting back in touch with their inner child was with the aid of hand puppets. Each had chosen a special puppet representative of their character, and often—especially when they thought that a conversation might become heated, they spoke to each other through their puppets. They said that along with finding it hard to get angry at cute characters, these playful, sometimes silly encounters often led to laughing out loud and then putting the puppets aside to enjoy spending time together.

Foreplay for the Fun of It

One of my clients recalled one of the nicest evenings she and her husband had during an overnight date at a hotel. She had booked a place that had a double Jacuzzi soaker tub in the bathroom and she'd packed bubble bath. After playing for an hour in the tub and emerging like prunes, they collapsed on the bed—exhausted. Not wanting to waste their time away together, they continued to caress one another and then, after spraying whipping cream on his penis, she pretended it was a lollipop and licked the cream off. By the time they were positioned for intercourse, they were both beyond pooped. They felt equally bad about not continuing to have sex as planned but decided instead to fall asleep in each other's arms. The hour and a half of exploring one another's bodies, enjoying their time together, and having fun did more to enhance their feeling of connectedness than five minutes of sex ever could.

As you and your partner continue to work at re-establishing intimacy, it's important to remember that a sexual experience is like a road trip. Mood setting, timing, foreplay, and intercourse itself are all stops along the way. Too many of us fall into thinking of intercourse as the ultimate destination. Try to take a moment to stop and think about how much pleasure you might be missing out on if you see mood setting and foreplay as simply means to an end. Sexual intercourse may indeed be one of the places you and your partner will visit, but the journey doesn't stop there either. Make sure you are taking the time to stop and smell all the roses. Your relationship will be better for it.

✳ HEIGHTENING THE CONNECTION ✳

In an effort to help create arousal and passion rather than wait for it to happen, some couples explore tantric or sacred sex. In an article for *Best Health Magazine*, Dr. Fraser shared the directions for an introductory tantric exercise:

"Begin by facing each other and gazing into each other's eyes—clothes on. Focus on one of your partner's eyes; this keeps you intimately exposed. (Some people look back and forth between the two eyes to reduce the tension, but that's cheating!) *Eyes are windows to the soul,* so you are gazing into his soul, he into yours. Next, synchronize your breathing: breathe in together, exhale together. Then move into breath exchange: you inhale when he exhales, then exhale when he inhales, as though you're breathing each other in. Practice this for at least ten minutes.

"To take this into sexual Tantra, try the same process but with clothes off. Sit on his lap, facing him, and wrap your legs around his waist. Do the breath exchange, but move into kissing and caressing. In time, begin slow intercourse, but continue caressing and kissing. Keep eye contact. *Here is where things get interesting; as you become more proficient, you can develop the ability for prolonged orgasm.* For both women and men, this is a variation on multiple orgasms; you remain at the peak of ecstatic pleasure without climaxing. There are all the feelings of a typical orgasm, but it lasts for many minutes (or even hours), without a traditional orgasm. *This leads to profound sexual and emotional merging,*" she writes.

Twelve

Keeping It Up

I'T'S ONE THING to get intimacy back on track; it's quite another to keep things going. This chapter will explore ways to keep intimacy and sex an ongoing priority in your marriage, and ways to spice things up. It will also take a look at some alternative lifestyles couples are dabbling in or choosing as an option.

Date Night

Valentine's Day was approaching and, resolute not to get swept up in the commercialism, I began looking for an *experience* that my husband and I could share together. After speaking to Carlyle Jansen and learning more about Good for Her, I signed us up for a February 13 workshop entitled Deepening Intimacy for Couples (tame by comparison to the Anal Sex and Tantric sex workshops!).

We left the kids with supper on the table and ventured to the house on Harbord Street in downtown Toronto that has been converted into a thriving business. Upon entering, we were met with a tasteful array of sexual paraphernalia to check out and purchase if we'd like. Up the steep staircase is where the workshops are held—a wooden floor, large area rug, and chairs in a circle serve as an inviting place to learn. Our entertaining, charismatic facilitator was none other than Carlyle herself. She was open, warm, and accepting and said all the right things to make us feel at home. She began by asking that we turn our phones to vibrate, so as not to be disrupted, and then with a smile requested that we "stick it between your legs." We all laughed, which loosened up those who were feeling a little apprehensive about attending—some because their partners had asked them to be there. I wondered about how many other workshop leaders could say that and get away with it. But hey, we were there to deepen intimacy and therefore talking about sexuality, and what turns us on, was par for the course.

That's about as "dirty" as Carlyle's talk got—she was mostly informative, great at setting the stage for the seven couples present to engage in dialogue with one another and to feel comfortable enough to share with the group what they were hoping to get out of the workshop. Carlyle shared that she has personally benefitted from teaching (and thus learning) about ways to deepen intimacy in her own relationships. She told us that she grew up in a home where her parents showed no intimacy. "I saw my mom kiss my dad—once, on the cheek," she shared. "And they slept in separate bedrooms." She's had to work hard at erasing her own blueprint for intimacy.

The couples ranged in age, anywhere from what appeared to be late twenties to early sixties. Most were heterosexual, but there were a couple of gay couples among us too. The couples had been living together (or been married) for as little as a year to more than thirty years. The common denominator was that we were all there to learn how to deepen our connection with our partners. For some, the connection was described as "good but could be better." For others, there was more of a disconnect, so they knew that they had to work harder at re-establishing intimacy. When asked to provide examples of how we share intimate moments, members of the group mentioned long walks together, deep conversations, holding hands, taking baths together, or cuddling on the couch.

Over the course of the workshop Carlyle gave us opportunities to talk to our partners about things we likely would not bring up at home. But because we were there to learn, and the environment was conducive to talking about intimacy, sex, and desire, that's what we did. We were asked to take turns asking each other seven questions, which included: "What first attracted you to me?"; "Has that attraction changed or not since then?"; "What do I do that gives you the most sexual pleasure?"; and "Is there anything I can do that works as an aphrodisiac for you?" She reminded us that the more we talked about what works for us, what we love and what we miss, the more intimacy we would build, the more desire we would feel for one another, and the more inclined we would be to bring pleasure to one another.

After being in our heads for a while, Carlyle led a series of playful activities designed to heighten our awareness of sensation—through both touch and movement. During one such activity, we took turns at being prey and predator and learned about what role we liked better. By the time the evening was wrapping up, I noticed that the majority of couples were noticeably more intimate. One had her legs casually draped over her partner, another was stroking her partner's back. I shared how much fun I'd had being playful and how I was looking forward to continuing to develop that side of myself.

I often ask couples in my counselling practice: "When was the last time you went on a date with one another?" Typically, they turn to look at one another, pause for a few seconds, and laugh. It's usually an embarrassed laugh; often, they can't remember the last time they spent time alone or left their kids with a babysitter and went out. Some will say that it's been months. Some say they never have. Others go out occasionally—often not alone, but with other couples. So, the idea of going on a date, just the two of them, is quite foreign. Yet most are not opposed to thinking and talking about the possibility.

Yes, it takes work and effort to change out of your sweatpants and T-shirt and into something a little less casual. Yes, it takes effort to put on a little lipstick or cologne. Yes, it takes work to brush your hair and arrange a babysitter or a place for the kids to stay overnight. And yes, it's worth the hassle. If you wait until the kids are old enough to stay in the house alone before you plan a night out, you're likely not going to have anything to say to one another! If you only go out with the girls or the guys for a few hours a week while your spouse stays at home with the kids, the kids miss out on seeing you dressed up and going out with just one another. This type of preparation and planning is an important way of saying, "You're worth it!" This is something your partner needs to hear, and something your kids can benefit from seeing modelled. So, try not to feel guilty when you leave them alone for a few hours with a babysitter. Enjoy your time together. Try not to talk about the kids while you are out (even though you may feel that the kids are all you have in common these days), and focus on remembering what it was like to spend quality time together when you first started dating. Once you start making time for each other in this way, my guess is that you'll begin to look forward to the next opportunity to spend time together, away from home and all its distractions. Luckily, there are countless ways you and your spouse can make date night fun and special.

The Conventional Date

The most conventional date I can think of is dinner and a movie—and that's 100 percent fine! It doesn't have to be a fancy restaurant, unless you both want it to be. Even something close to home and informal is better than cooking and cleaning up after yourselves, right? I know that it's easier (and less expensive) to wait until you can access the new release in your living room, but there's something magical about seeing characters on a really big screen and sharing a bag of popcorn together.

Don't fall into the trap of thinking that Saturday is your only option for dating. If you're both self-employed (or have flexible work schedules) and the kids are at school, what about doing away with the need for a babysitter and going for lunch and a matinee while they're occupied? If the kids are old enough to stay at home alone, what about checking out an art exhibit on a Sunday afternoon or window shopping on a sunny Saturday? Maybe pretend to be tourists in your own city and do the hop on, hop off the bus thing.

Women, who have either been assigned or have assumed the role of social director, often really appreciate taking turns when it comes to planning dates. So, even if you're only managing to connect as a couple once a month or every second weekend, take turns. Maybe set a budget so that neither is angry at the other for planning something too extravagant.

And if you're stumped about where to go and what to do, consider searching online. One particularly helpful resource specifically for couples is www.2life.io. What began in 2004 as *2couples*—a print magazine—has since evolved into a digital magazine with lots of great information and advice. In 2013, they introduced an app not just for couples but for any two people who share a special or important relationship. Diane Hall, founder of the magazine and site, describes the app as "the fridge in your pocket." In other words, "It's where you communicate about your day, co-ordinate events, share pictures and lists." The app evolved out of Diane's belief (one I share) that "being a good partner" is key and "if you're communicating well with your partner, then you'll feel closer and intimacy between you will be strengthened."

Diane was quick to mention that the app is not meant to replace verbal communication, but she recognizes that communication via technology, even between couples, has become very commonplace.

We chatted about how much impact social media has had on

relationships. How about yours? When you last read an interesting article online, saw something interesting in your travels, experienced a first with your child, or received an exciting phone call, whom did you share this with first? I suspect that many of you might have spread the news to your Twitter followers or Facebook friends before sharing it with your partner. Consider what happens when you share so much of your day with others, some even strangers to you, instead of with your spouse. When you come together at the end of your day, you may not remember what it was you were excited about reading or thinking earlier, or even feel the need anymore to share it. Over time, this habit of sharing with others first can lead to a huge disconnect. An app such as the one on the 2life site can bring sharing back home, ensuring that you and your spouse are the first "go to" people in each other's lives, and providing an intimate spot to connect with one another during your time apart.

The app has gained international attention. Although the content is in English, the tools are available in fourteen languages. So far, their number one market is in the US. Canada is second, followed by Japan, and the number of users is growing monthly.

Not surprisingly, the app even offers a "date night" section. Each week, there's a new idea. Whether you're inspired by the idea or not, you can invite your partner to any scheduled event through a shared calendar.

The At-Home Date

Carlyle Jansen often talks to the couples in her workshops about ways of creating shared experiences. "If we are just talking about each other's days and our own private lives, we are not creating shared experiences," she says. And she doesn't believe you always have to go out to do this. She suggests that couples "create date nights where they stay in. Often, after they go out to a movie and come home at eleven, they're too tired to be intimate with one another," she says. "So stay in."

If you're parenting young children, part of your planning would, of course, include finding friends or relatives with whom they could spend the night. Some couples with similar or same-aged children organize a co-operative of sorts, where they exchange overnight babysitting with one another. That way, the kids get to spend time with their friends and two couples benefit from the arrangement. If the kids are curious about what you're going to be doing while they are out, just tell them that you're going to spend time focusing on each other. That's all they need to hear as an important message: that their parents care about and value their relationship.

If your children are teens and generally out of the house a fair amount, they'd likely be thrilled to have their curfew delayed to accommodate your plans (although they may say that you're "too old" and that it's kind of weird and creepy that you actually want to spend time alone—yuck!).

And once they've left the nest, of course, you'll have more time than you need on your hands. Unfortunately, if you haven't kept the romance, fun, and positive feelings towards one another burning, then your relationship is at risk of turning to ash at this time.

Staying at home allows you to draw from numerous resources to stimulate your bodies and your senses—items such as candles, bubble bath, and massage oil. If you don't have all the accessories on hand, you may need to purchase some ahead of time, perhaps during one of your dates outside of the house.

Even though it may seem contrived to plan something special indoors, and even if it's very easy to get sidetracked by the sound of an incoming text or phone call, try to ignore these interruptions. After a little bit of initial awkwardness, you will likely relax and wonder why you didn't do this sooner.

✻ "SEX"CESSORIES ✻

So-called adult toys (once referred to as marital aids) are great accessories to have on hand. *Toronto Life* magazine's 2013 sex poll revealed that "77 percent of women and 68 percent of men have tried toys or use them occasionally or routinely."

Vibrators, for example, need not be used only by women during masturbation. When integrated into lovemaking, they can touch on and amplify the intensity of an orgasm for women as well as men. A woman can introduce a vibrator as an accessory to her male partner by rolling it against and behind his testicles, against his perineum (or anus), or even playing with it on his nipples. She can also suggest that he use the toy on her.

Another option is the We-Vibe. According to information on their website, "she wears it during sex for extra stimulation to her clitoris and G-spot. Together you both share the vibe." It is, according to the site, "the world's no. 1 couple's vibrator."

Other options for enhancing your experience could include:

- strap-on harnesses
- butt plugs and beads
- floggers, whips, and paddles
- blindfolds and collars
- other kinky accessories

The Get-Away Date

As a special treat, instead of staying home or going out on a date, some couples find that vacationing together—even for a night or two—can reignite an old spark. Even spending a night at a hotel in your own city (maybe one with a soaker tub big enough for two) and then enjoying breakfast in bed can rejuvenate you individually and as a couple.

If you're planning on going away without the kids, it's often more relaxing and conducive to "we" time to choose a destination for adults only. It doesn't have to be kinky or erotic (unless you want it to), but you're unlikely to want to go to a family-oriented hotel if you've chosen not to take your kids along.

There are many to choose from. If you're simply looking to have a quiet time away with your partner, a mainstream couples-only resort such as Couples Resort in Algonquin Park, Ontario, is a great idea. If you're looking for more of a titillating time away, you may want to consider a clothing-optional resort (or check out Bare Necessities Tour and Travel, an agency in Austin, Texas, that has organized nude travel experiences since 1990).

John Sorensen, owner of Couples Resort, says that theirs is "a resort for couples without the kids—clean and simple." Many of their rooms have double Jacuzzis, walk-in showers with multiple heads, and wood-burning fireplaces. Some even have steam baths in the room, saunas in the bathroom, and hot tubs on their decks.

Other than their semi-formal five-course dining experience, there are no planned evening activities, says Sorensen, because the couples are there to make their own fun, not to get to know others.

Taking It Up a Notch

Some couples are happy to enjoy the simple pleasures of getting reacquainted with one another in the comfort of their own home, while others are looking for something a little more adventurous. For these couples, an at-home or conventional date just doesn't make the grade. Perhaps they're both open to something a little more intoxicating, a little more alternative. But even alternative lifestyles are moving towards becoming mainstream nowadays. Let's explore some.

Out in the Open

The dinner plates had been cleared at a friend's home and dessert was on the table when our conversation moved in the direction of alternative lifestyles. Soon, everyone was engaged in animated discussion about other people's sex lives, and even making subtle inferences about their own. It was interesting, but not surprising, to hear the divide between husbands and their wives. At first, the men were quieter but the women could tell what they were thinking by the way they were smirking at one another. The women were more vocal—one said that even the thought of having sex with someone else present or swapping partners at a party felt like a violation of their relationship.

The host shared a story about how for years she had thought that the loud music and line of cars on her street was coming from the corner house where teenagers lived with their parents. She imagined that the parents went away on weekends and left the older teenagers to fend for themselves. Then one day, while standing outside discussing this with another neighbour, she was surprised to learn that the party house was not the one she thought, but the one next door, where a couple in their fifties, whose children were away at university, lived. The music and traffic was as a result of their weekend swingers parties—where guests were encouraged to flirt and have sex with people other than the partners they had come to the party with, either by choice or as a result of randomly picking his or her keys or watch out of a bowl in the front entrance.

My friend, the hostess, was surprised that the affluent, well-manicured street on which she lived (she joked about finally understanding why it is known as one of the "most desirable" streets in her neighbourhood) held parties of this sort, but with my increasingly growing fund of information about adults wanting to explore more open alternative sexual lifestyles, I was able to confidently share that swinging among consenting adults—rich and poor, well educated and not so much—was very much alive and well (dare I say up and coming?) and living not only on the quiet street of her seemingly conservative neighbourhood, but in many bedroom communities across North America and beyond.

Curious to learn more about neighbourhood swinger houses, the husbands at the dinner party were half-jokingly asking where they could sign up and the women were left wondering how couples living in the same neighbourhood, potentially with kids attending school together, could "get away with it," and asking, "Don't the wives get jealous?"

The discussion continued until it was time to say good night, but may have continued between each couple as they drove back home. Perhaps it served as a great springboard towards opening up discussion about whether or not they might consider this or other ways to enhance their own sex lives.

Swinging

Swinging is not a new lifestyle. It used to be called wife swapping until that term was considered too sexist. It was even written about under the section of "further out" practices in the 1972 bestselling book, *The Joy of Sex*. But swinging is not confined to people's homes as it once may have been. No matter the city in which you live, there is no shortage of options for couples venturing into swinging on an experimental basis or as a lifestyle choice—from neighbourhood gatherings to swinging clubs (also known as sex clubs or lifestyle clubs).

* CURTIS AND YVONNE *

After Curtis and Yvonne had taken turns at planning evenings out or at home with one another over a course of a few months, they found that there was a greater connection between them. However, Yvonne still worried about why she wasn't feeling much inclination to have sex with Curtis. She wasn't sure if this was because it had become monotonous or if, at the age of forty-eight, she was losing her desire to be sexual with anyone.

She'd read about the positive experiences some people had at swingers clubs and asked Curtis if he'd be willing to go with her on their next date. At first he was quite apprehensive. He too had heard about these "sex positive" clubs but had never ventured into one. She hadn't either but was excited to share the experience with him. Wanting to make Yvonne happy, Curtis agreed to try it at least once.

After paying their entrance fee for the evening, they joined other couples who were "fraternizing," dancing, and drinking on the lower-level "foreplay dance floor," as Yvonne put it. Since they had to pay an additional fee to get naked and go upstairs to a private area with round beds and hot tubs, they declined this on their first visit.

Their first experience was very positive. Yvonne remembered everyone being very "friendly" and that it was a "fun" night. "It was a very suggestive environment and the dress code was quite different to what you'd find at a regular bar or club. Some of the women were even wearing lingerie. Most were dressed quite scantily," she said. Yvonne found the environment very stimulating and exciting. "Anything goes, so I could grind up against Curtis and no one would think there was anything wrong with that. Curtis wasn't in the least bit interested in being with anyone else, and although I was more open to it, I appreciated his being there with me so I didn't want to push it."

When they returned a couple of months later, the club had changed its policy. With no additional fee required now to venture onto the upper floor, they agreed to check it out. "We had to take our street clothes off and put them in a locker," she said. "We were allowed to wrap a towel around our bodies and so we did. We found a round bed and started making out. I found it incredibly erotic and stimulating knowing that other couples were doing the same all around us. I was also turned on by knowing that others were watching us." Yvonne shared that although other couples approached them at various times to ask if they could join in, they said no, and that was cool, since rules around respect and consent are strongly adhered to at swingers clubs.

I was curious to know if their occasional visits to swingers clubs had translated into more passion at home. Yvonne laughed. "Well," she said, "it's like going out for a great dinner. You enjoy it. You have a fantastic time, but then the following night you're eating chicken at home. The best thing about going to the club is that it reassured me that it wasn't menopause or the fact that the relationship was older that made sex less exciting. I realized that I needed a booster or something a little bit different to keep me turned on. I was so happy to know that I wasn't losing my mojo and that even a change of environment was enough to get the flow happening."

Although Yvonne and Curtis have gone to the club several times, Yvonne stresses that they have not chosen swinging as a lifestyle. Their experiments with swinging are just an occasional diversion from the ordinary—a way to spice up their relationship—and she insists that neither of them has any interest in being with other people.

✳ DON'T LOSE YOURSELF ✳

When Curtis joined Yvonne at the swingers club, despite it not really being his scene, I believe he was demonstrating what Dr. Amy Muise calls "high sexual communal strength." Sexual communal strength (SCS), for the studies with which she is involved, is defined as the motivation to meet a partner's sexual needs. Other more commonly mentioned activities that people engage in so as to meet their partner's needs are: having sex when it is not personally desired (but because they know that their partner will feel happy or loved more as a result), engaging in a sexual act or position that one's partner is into, even though it may not be your favourite, and being open-minded, non-judgmental, and responsive when your partner shares his or her sexual interests or fantasies, even if you don't engage in them. Dr. Muise and her colleagues have found that people high in sexual communal strength, and their partners, report higher sexual desire (and the ability to maintain desire over the course of time in their relationships) as well as higher relationship and sexual satisfaction.

However, she cautions about going too far when wanting to meet a partner's sexual needs. This she refers to as "sexual unmitigated communion" or SUC, which is the focus on a partner's needs at the exclusion of one's own.

So, I'm thinking that if Curtis's going to the swinging club is an example of SUC rather than high SCS, then it would not yield the same benefits and could even lead to negative sexual experiences, such as feeling more distracted, more disconnected, bored, or apathetic during sex.

"In other words," says Dr. Muise, "being motivated to meet a partner's sexual needs seems to have benefits, so long as people do not lose sight of their own desires in the process."

Yvonne and Curtis are not alone in their desire to explore the alternative lifestyle that swinging offers. The demographics of people at swinging clubs are broad. There are single males— usually more single men than women because "men tend to be more open to this lifestyle because they are horny, want to get laid and have fun," says Matt Poirier, owner of Club 4M—a popular swinging destination in Etobicoke, Ontario—and single females (because the club is not just for the majority of members who come as couples) looking to hook up with other singles or married couples from every sexual orientation and across a large age range—from mid-twenties to mid-seventies. Matt says that the average age of couples that come to the club is around forty. He guesses this is because it's around that time that they've been together for ten or more years and are looking for "a way to spice things up."

And they come in all shapes and sizes—from could-be models to people who have to turn sideways to get in the door, he says. With their clothes off, there's nothing to distinguish the janitor from the judge or the student from the medical doctor. There are no expensive suits or flashy jewellery to separate the have and the have-nots. Matt says that most of the swinging couples have kids, a college or university education, have been married for a number of years, and are medium-to-high income earners. Everyone is there for the same reason—to explore and play.

There's no pressure to engage in anything that you don't want to do. There are also no limitations as to who can be with whom. "It's about freedom of choice and freedom of expression," says Matt. "There are three basic rules of our club: consent, respect and discretion." Follow this and everything else is up to you. You can have sex with others without being in love with them; you can have sex with the one you love. You can have sex with one other person or two or three or more. But if you can't abide by the rules, you will be asked to leave.

Matt—who has embraced the lifestyle along with the business opportunity—says he couldn't be happier. When he and his wife started to experiment with swinging, they simply had sex with one another in what Matt calls a very "sexually conducive" environment. Eventually, this evolved into having others join them. Matt says that he enjoys watching his wife have sex with other people and that "the hottest sex we've ever had is after having sex with other people [for some, the thought or vision of their partner with someone else arouses their desire to be with him or her] and if I want to have sex with another girl, I don't have to hide it from my wife."

Matt says that he is able to clearly separate his sexual infidelity from his loyalty to his wife in all other parts of their lives together. He considers himself to be a faithful and loyal husband and feels fortunate because he believes that she does not feel threatened, jealous, or insecure.

So, with all this open communication and willingness to accept others into their relationship, I asked Matt if they ever experience difficulties in their sex life.

"Of course," he responds. "Do we still have nights when I want to have sex and she doesn't, or vice versa? Yes. I am not advocating swinging as a miracle solution or a little blue pill. All I'm saying is that this lifestyle has opened us up and helped us. And if we were to rate how satisfying our sexual life is compared to most other couples', we would score a lot higher. However, we don't score perfect."

Matt and his wife are clearly experiencing the upside of the swinging lifestyle, but my advice is that if you're considering venturing down this road, do so with your eyes wide open. One of the problems with swinging (or any type of casual sex or hooking up just for the fun of it) is that people's feelings often get hurt. On his everyonelovessex.org site, Pastor Bryan Sands posts a regular blog about sexual faithfulness. In one, titled "Sex and Glue: The emotional bond of a physical act," he quotes from *Change Your Brain, Change Your Life*, by Dr. Daniel Amen (a prominent American psychiatrist and brain disorders expert):

Whenever a person is sexually involved with another person, neurochemical changes occur in both their brains that encourage limbic, emotional bonding. Yet limbic bonding is the reason casual sex doesn't really work for most people on a whole mind and body level. Two people may decide to have sex "just for the fun of it," yet something is occurring on another level they might not have decided on at all: sex is enhancing an emotional bond between them whether they want it or not. One person, often the woman, is bound to form an attachment and will be hurt when a casual affair ends. One reason it is usually the woman who is hurt most is that the female limbic system is larger than the male's.

This passage highlights the risks of having sex with others "just for the fun of it." Despite having no intention to take it further or to feel any type of bond or connection, your feelings may have a mind of their own, so to speak.

Sands writes in his blog that, "Even though casual sex is extremely common nowadays, the partners involved in the act are creating a significant bond. I would be as bold to say 'casual sex' is not possible because of the bond that is created."

When speaking to Matt about casual sex, I wonder out loud about husbands or wives being exposed to a lifestyle where he or she might be lured away from the marriage. Matt shares statistics from the Kinsey Institute indicating that divorce rates for open and swinging couples are lower than those who are in monogamous relationships. He believes that engaging in sexual fantasies and desires together is far better than cheating behind one another's backs. However, he admits that "to pretend that nothing like that [partners leaving the relationship for others they have met at the club] ever happens would be untrue."

Bottom line? It's very important to weigh the benefits of a swinging lifestyle (or visits to a club) alongside the risks to your marriage, and to consider the possible outcomes if things don't go according to plan. For example, what happens if what begins as mutual curiosity ends in conflict and hurt? What if one of you wants to pull out and the other says, "Hang on a minute. I'm enjoying this." What then?

And even if *you* never go back to the club again, is it possible that your partner might? What about setting the bar too high, and then feeling that your partner is expecting too much from you?

Before you set foot in a swinging environment or engage in any alternative sexual lifestyle, my advice is to be sure to think this through carefully—alone and together. Don't approach with reckless abandon or just for fun. Don't jump on the bandwagon without discussion and pre-planning. Create clear boundaries and communicate your goals.

Kink and Fetishism

Remember when you were a child and loved to dress up and role-play with your friends? Maybe you were the teacher and your friend the student. Maybe you were the wife and your friend the husband. Well, you can enjoy a different kind of role-playing as an adult too. Sexual play can be as tame as using feathers to tickle and tantalize one another and as wild as dressing up as a dominatrix in leather and handcuffing your submissive partner to the bed. So long as the play is consensual and safe, (a "safe word" is often suggested as a way of allowing the "submissive" to communicate his or her desire to stop or tone it down to the "dominant" partner), the sky's the limit.

Those who are into BDSM (a variety of erotic practices involving dominance and submission, role-playing, and restraint), fetishism, or kink take it quite seriously. The three appear to be intertwined and are often offshoots of each other. Fetlife.com, for example, is a free social networking site run by "kinksters" for other kinksters (or those who are curious) to seek out others with similar interests in a wide range of BDSM or kinky activities. The site lists the locations of "munches"—relaxed social gatherings in public places such as a bar or restaurant where like-minded people can interact in a no-pressure environment.

As with swinging, the key to experimenting with any form of "kink" is open communication. How far do you and your partner want to go? Is being spanked or tied up enough or too much?

How would you feel about indulging a foot fetish with a bit of whipped cream? It's important for both partners to be honest about their feelings so that a mutual decision can be made about further exploration or pulling back. Some married couples approach these lifestyles on an experimental basis, try something once, and never try it again. Others may really enjoy the outcome and embrace the practice.

Polyamory

The first time I heard about polyamory was when a client told me that his twenty-six-year-old son was involved in a romantic relationship with another couple, with whom he lived. He avoided visiting them because he found it all very "strange" and "uncomfortable" to be around. Serendipitously, the television show *Polyamory* aired a couple of weeks later, so I was able to get a further glimpse into this lifestyle. *Polyamory* means *many loves*. It's different than swinging, because the three or more polyamorous individuals consider themselves committed to each other in a relationship, whereas swingers typically go home with their significant other.

Although polyamorous relationships are still considered fringe, there are more people engaged in them now than there were a decade ago. A *Toronto Life* article titled "Sex without Borders" explored this multi-partner lifestyle. Writer Courtney Shea interviewed Stephane and Samantha, who are apparently Toronto's best-known advocates for polyamory (Toronto is known as one of the most poly-friendly places in North America). After corresponding with Samantha myself, I learned that she and Stephane met in 2001, married in 2004, and have had an open relationship since 2006. In the polyamory world, they are known as a "primary couple," but have sexual relationships with "lower ranking" lovers.

In 2011, Samantha founded the Toronto-based all weekend annual conference on sexuality and relationships, called Playground. On her website, notyourmothersplayground.com, Samantha tells us more about her book of the same name. She writes: "With the innocent days of key parties and free love behind us, *Not Your Mother's Playground: A Realistic Guide to Honest, Happy, and Healthy Open Relationships* is a how-to guide for navigating today's very different world of modern-day non-monogamy. From swinging to polyamory, it walks readers through the many ups and downs they may encounter along their journey."

Each month, hundreds of members of a group named Polyamory Toronto get together to discuss issues such as how to talk to their families about their lifestyle and how to deal with jealousy. There are polyamory groups in cities all across Canada, the United States, and beyond.

Polygamy

With shows such as *My Five Wives* and *Sister Wives* being so popular, we are either extremely curious, living vicariously through lifestyles that appear more interesting than our own, or on the lookout for alternate lifestyles to explore! At first, I was confused. Why would any woman want to be only one of five, for example, married to the same man? I learned, however, that for the most part, this lifestyle is not one that the women have chosen, but rather one that they were born into. Most have been raised in polygamist families where they are taught to believe, follow, and uphold certain doctrines. So, while it might be nice for the man to be king and have his choice of several wives to sleep with, this lifestyle, it seems, is mostly based on beliefs about not wasting a man's seed and allowing him to procreate with many women so as to propagate.

I also wondered, at first, if part of the appeal for women in this lifestyle was the ability to share the workload. However, when watching *My Five Wives*, I realized that each has more than her fair share of work. Each is essentially a single mom, with the father flitting from home to home and bed to bed. The women, despite their strong beliefs about their lifestyle and their mostly encouraging support of one another, still experience real human emotions such as jealousy and feelings of competitiveness—almost as if they are siblings competing for a father's attention. Of all the alternate lifestyles I have explored in this chapter, I'm thinking that this is the least likely to become widespread.

—

After reading this chapter, it may come as no surprise to learn that non-monogamous behaviour has many supporters in this age of sexual exploration and liberation. While it may still be mainstream to strive towards a committed sexual relationship with a primary partner, I can't help but wonder what the future holds for our children with regard to monogamous behaviour and how marriage and family will be defined. With so many people looking outside their monogamous relationships to have their sexual needs met, and so many marriages ending in divorce, often as a result of infidelity, more couples may ultimately explore the option of consenting to one another's sexual engagement with others (together and apart) as a way of avoiding divorce and emotions related to discovering infidelity.

When considering your own relationship, and how far you are willing or tempted to go in order to spice things up, think carefully about the long-term consequences for yourself, your partner, and your children (if you have them). An at-home date night that includes massage oil and handcuffs is a world away from trips to swinging clubs. A cozy weekend away at an adult-only resort is very different from hooking up with strangers at a sexy beach resort in Mexico. As always, open and honest communication in the present can prevent heartache and turmoil down the road.

Thirteen

When Things Don't Improve

S O, YOU'VE READ all about excuses and understand the real reasons you're not having sex.
You've even tried to engage your spouse, sometimes more successfully than others, in the exercises and suggestions for ways to
spice things up. Along the journey, one or both of you have been
open to change and, at other times, resistant. Still, you notice that
there has not been much movement—in either direction. It's as
if you're in neutral, just gliding along. And your sex life has not
shown much improvement. In this chapter we will explore some
possibilities as to why you have not seen much change, some very
valid reasons you will likely want to continue forging ahead, and
the options that lie before you right now.

The way I see it, you have a few options: you can either stay
as you are, you can persevere with working towards change, or
you can decide to part ways. Change requires continued hard
work and patience, motivation, and courage. Change comes in
the form of everything from adjusting your expectations in the
marriage to exploring alternative lifestyles, and lots in between.
If you stay as you are, you may already be living in or heading

towards a miserable marriage. The problem with staying unhappily married is that everyone suffers. You may become physically or mentally unwell over time and your children are robbed of seeing a healthy, happy relationship modelled for them. In addition, since even mostly happily married people find themselves thinking about or engaged in sexual relationships outside of their marriage, even when they believe it to be totally out of character, unhappily married people are even more vulnerable to emotional or physical affairs—whether they're actively seeking them or not.

The last option is to consider parting ways. Truly, this should be your last option, especially since there are so many possibilities for making things better.

Why Change?

In my practice, I have heard similar themes emerge in regards to why couples want to work towards change.

"We want a better connection."

The most common reason that couples share for wanting to improve their sex life is that they want a better connection. They say that they have noticed a direct relationship between the amount of sex they are having and the degree of emotional connection between them. Without sex as a connector, they say that they have drifted apart and communicate less—especially about deeper feelings and thoughts. In other words, they are feeling a loss of intimacy or closeness.

As we've learned, research has shown that there is indeed a connection between sexual intimacy and intimacy in general.

This is why I sometimes suggest that couples put the cart before the horse and have sex even when they aren't feeling particularly inspired. It seems that intimacy begets intimacy, and having sex can open the door to communication.

"I'm afraid of fracturing our family."

Fear is a powerful motivator. If you've been married for a number of years, and have built a life together, it's only natural to worry about putting it all at risk. The good news is that if you are worried about ending your relationship and disrupting your family, chances are that this is not the outcome you want. Thinking about and being aware of everything you have to lose can be a powerful motivator to work towards change.

"We want to be positive role models for the kids."

Although children may not know the specifics of your sexual relationship, they are quick to pick up on ways—good and bad—that each of you talk to and treat the other or may even overhear a conversation that one of you is having with a friend about your sex life. Other than sex, children learn about intimacy and connection from the way they see you interact. For many couples, this knowledge is a very powerful motivator of change.

"We feel that an improved sex life will improve our overall health."

Sex does improve overall health. There are absolutely short- and long-term physical and emotional health improvements that come from having a healthy sex life. If you're not convinced—or if this wasn't on your list of motivators—consider the following:

- The longer you abstain from sex, the lower your hormone and sperm or egg production. You ultimately lose your sexual chemistry potential, and that affects your health.

- People who no longer have sexual intimacy in their lives tend to develop a range of health disorders, both physical and mental, more readily than those who remain sexually active.

- Individuals in long-term sexually intimate relationships live longer than most other people.

- Sexual activity reduces depression and anger, anxiety, and stress.

- Ovarian and prostate cancer are related to infrequency of sexual release.[1]

And, according to other research, it turns out that for both men and women, there is truth to the old adage "use it or lose it!"

- On average, men get three to five erections per night in addition to erections that result from sexual activity. Dr. Ajay Nehra, a professor of urology at the Mayo College of Medicine, says erections are important for penile muscle health because they bring much-needed oxygen to the penis. This helps maintain the health of the nerves—making sex a healthy habit.

- A Finnish study showed that men who had sex once a week were half as likely to develop erectile dysfunction as men who had sex less frequently. In women, more frequent sex also stimulates circulation to the genitals. In turn, this enhances lubrication and the elasticity of vaginal tissues—both of which go a long way toward boosting a woman's enjoyment of sex.[2]

"It's my obligation or duty."

Depending on the home in which you were raised, a woman may believe that it is her duty to keep her husband happy. She may have seen this modelled by her mother, or it may be even further entrenched, in the roots of her culture or religion. This motivator has less to do with satisfying oneself (as a woman), and more to do with following through with the doctrines by which previous generations have lived. Although this may be a valid reason to want to improve your sex life, if having sex does not leave you satisfied or if you have become emancipated by moving to a new country or as a result of what you have learned, you may be less motivated over time.

What's in Your Way?

Finding your motivating force and reminding yourself of the good reasons you want to change can keep you moving in a positive direction, even when you're getting weary. But sometimes you have to look a bit deeper.

When I work with a couple over a period of months but notice that there is not much change, this is how I help them to look for the things that may be standing in their way: I ask them to think about the process that they are engaged in as a journey, and to name the boulders that might be stopping them from moving further down the road. When I understand the boulders that are preventing them from reaching their goals, I can help them push the heavy rocks out of the way so their path is clearer.

The most common boulders are probably the most obvious: financial troubles, arguments over how to raise the kids, et cetera. But after everything you've read here, you likely realize that excuses are boulders too, and they often require a lot of strength and effort to push aside.

In counselling sessions, I am always curious to hear and see who wants to remove the boulders and who would prefer to keep them in place. If one partner is working hard at trying to remove a boulder but the other partner is not putting in much effort, this is an important reflection of where the unwilling partner stands. If you feel that you're the only one working towards change, then say what you're feeling out loud. Let your partner know if you're not prepared to do this alone.

Sometimes, the unwilling partner has already left the path and is moving down another on his own (or with someone new). He may be involved in a relationship with someone outside the marriage and, therefore, has no desire or incentive to walk down the path together. Or, perhaps one partner sees the boulders as a form of protection. Maybe she has travelled down the path with her partner for many years, but over time, has been hurt or let down so many times that the boulders are now barriers she prefers to leave as is so that she cannot be reached. Deciding whether or not to remove these boulders is often a difficult task and may require professional help.

The other question I often ask couples is: "If we were to remove the boulders so you could walk more freely and in union on the same path towards a destination, what would that destination look like?" This question often reveals an interesting fact: boulders can serve as a couple's way of avoiding confrontation and divisiveness. But once the boulders are taken away, they can no longer avoid discussing the destination and they may find that they have very different goals. One partner may want to retire in a warm climate when their children have left the nest, and the other may feel panicked at living apart from their adult children. Sometimes, the "destination" is not as literal. Perhaps it's having more sex and increased intimacy, and the boulders have made it possible for the couple to avoid discussing a touchy subject. By the time they come to see me, they may have spent years arguing about their sexual problems (or pushing them aside and getting nowhere). All of the rocks (excuses) thrown in the path have metaphorically morphed into one large boulder, which is now so heavy and so dense that it's almost impossible to move. Instead of instructing the couple to exert all their energy into moving the massive roadblock, I provide each person with tools to chisel away at the boulder's formation and then to examine and identify each rock to see what lies beneath it.

At the core of the biggest boulders is generally a smouldering mix of toxic emotions—anger, fear, resentment, pain, disappointment, sadness—all contributing to a lack of desire for close physical proximity. Only after these emotions are exposed and examined can the couple begin moving towards a more sexually satisfying life together.

Do You Both Want to Change?

Sometimes I notice that one partner is well prepared with notes and reminders brought to the session, whereas the other is behaving as if the only thing he or she has to do is show up on time and interact with me and his or her partner, and their sex life will magically improve. Of course, if only one partner is motivated, change is unlikely. The working partner will come to resent working alone and may not understand why he or she is not getting any help.

In order for change to occur, there absolutely has to be motivation on both sides. You've probably heard the saying "You can lead a horse to water, but you cannot make him drink." The same is true here. I can lead you to knowing more about why married couples don't have sex, but I can't force change, unless you want it. And most important, both of you need to want it if real change is going to take place.

Here, then, are some common reasons that a partner may not be on board or working towards change:

- There may already be someone waiting in the wings.
- A partner may have an undisclosed separate agenda. They may be biding time by coming to sessions because they don't have their ducks in a row, but do have plans to leave the relationship once everything is firmed up.
- A partner may benefit from keeping things just as they are. For example, he may not have to put in any extra time or effort to maintain the status quo. He may not even be as desirous as he once was to have sex and so is actually okay with the lack thereof, even though he tells her otherwise.
- There were concerns that haunted one or both of the partners even before they married, and these concerns have become more of an issue over time. For example, a large age spread between partners may not seem to be much of a problem at twenty-five and thirty-five, but later on, the divide can appear bigger as energy levels and interests change for one partner and not the other. Or a couple who met in high school, dated only each other, and married ten years after meeting may regret not having dated more or realize that they might have chosen a different partner later on in life. One partner or the other may not really have wanted to get married in the first place. Perhaps theirs was an arranged marriage (against their will), or nagging, negative intuitive feelings were ignored and labelled as wedding day jitters.

- One partner or the other may be experiencing medical issues that prevent them from enjoying increased intimacy. As discussed earlier, a trip to the family doctor can help establish if there are health concerns that should be addressed.

- One partner or the other may have unresolved issues about their own sexuality.

Looking Deeper

Even when both partners are on board, there are factors that can influence a couple's ability to realize their goals. If you don't see any change, even after understanding the real reasons you're not having sex, consider the questions below to see where else you might be stuck:

Answer yes or no to the following:

1. Is your partner so "badly behaved" that you can't bear to be with him/her?

2. Are you finding your partner physically unattractive?

3. Do you feel that your partner is too sexually demanding of you?

4. Do you feel that your partner spends too much time on electronics and not enough time with you?

5. Do either you or your partner have a physical or mental health issue that impedes your ability or desire to have sex?

6. Have you found ways to spice up your sex life?

7. Are you spending more time together—date nights, for example?

8. Are you spending more time on foreplay so that you are sufficiently aroused before having sex?

9. Are you both working hard at setting the right mood for lovemaking?

10. Are you communicating your sexual needs? What you do and don't like?

Once you've had an opportunity to respond to each of these questions, share your responses with one another. See if you're on the same page and, if not, discuss why not and what you'd like to improve. If you find that your partner is resistant to discussing these ten questions and responses or resistant to change in general, then perhaps one of the more common reasons that I described above—as to why your partner is not on board—is at play.

Does a Sexless Marriage = Divorce?

If you have made your way through all of the tips and exercises and suggestions in this chapter and others, and are still finding that you're not making progress or that your partner is unwilling to work at change, it may be time to ask yourself some hard questions. Is this an acceptable way for you to live? Even though some women joke about being relieved at not having to "put out," is this really so? It's nice to know that sex is there when you want it, so what if that option is no longer available? Can you live the rest of your life with your partner? And if things don't improve, is your relationship doomed?

In a 2009 *New York Times* article, Denise A. Donnelly—an associate professor of sociology at Georgia State University who has studied sexless marriage—shared that she has found that people in sexless marriages were more likely to have considered divorce and were less happy than those in sexually active marriages.

She also reports on feedback from respondents who have kept in touch with her: "The happiest ones are actually those that have moved on to other partners," she says. "It may be that lack of sex is a signal that all intimacy in a marriage is over, and that both would be happier in other situations."[3]

Divorce, however, is certainly not the only option for couples who are living in sexless marriages. Many couples have comfortable and happy platonic relationships; it may not be ideal, but it may be better than splitting up, for many reasons. Ultimately, it's a question of what works for both of you, and what you are both comfortable with over the long haul.

Conclusion

The Destination

So, HERE I SIT, months after my journey began. The foreplay, as it turns out, was my attendance at the Mother and Babies Salsa group, and it was followed by many months of research and mental masturbation before I even began writing! Along the journey, I have reached many climaxes (when my thoughts came together well) and valleys (like when I lost an entire chapter somewhere in my computer and stayed up until 2 a.m. with my daughter, who eventually found it in some remote location!). My lover—my partner—during the writing of this manuscript has been the words on my screen, at times caressing and flowing through me as smoothly as a bubbling brook on a warm spring day, and at other times resistant and unwilling to change. Putting the final chapter together is always a time of sadness and elation for me. In some ways, it is like saying farewell to a familiar lover—one I have come to depend on daily for comfort and companionship. On the other hand, there is a sense of elation at having come this far, and at being able to share what I have learned with my readers. And, as with satisfying sex, I look forward to basking in its afterglow, as well as maintaining my desire to educate others through my words.

A lot has changed for me personally while writing this book. I have become more aware of the messages I received about sex as I was growing up and how they were reinforced by my mother as I became an adult. After she passed away, I was more able to distance myself from these messages and reflect on the effect they have had on me. In doing so, I have come to realize how important it is for me not to pass the same messages on to my daughters. I want them to know that as long as they're mature enough to understand the consequences of giving oneself completely, and have partners who treat them well, sex should be fun and playful and not something that they're afraid to embrace and enjoy.

Writing this book has allowed me to springboard into great discussions with my daughters about sex and condoms and boys and dating and relationships, not necessarily in that order. It's also opened up discussions about feeling comfortable with exploring one's body through masturbation and knowing what feels good before being able to let others know about their needs and desires. We've discussed sex before marriage and I've shared with my older daughter that there may be benefits to her having sex with more than one man in her entire life so as to know what her sexual preferences are before she settles into a monogamous relationship, if that is what she chooses.

My belief that monogamy is difficult to maintain has also been reinforced through the writing of this book.

I have come to recognize, with increasing value, the importance of play, of having fun with and connecting with one's partner regularly, and I hope that you will, by reading this book, have recognized this too. I now know of resources and have knowledge of accessories to enhance playful encounters.

I have also come to see that regardless of lessons learned from our parents and the culture in which we are raised, sex and the desire to engage in intimacy with other human beings are normal—in fact, primal urges. One only has to look at nature to find hundreds of examples of this. Put a male and female rabbit in a cage and their basic instinct is to mate. In fact, the sexual act actually triggers ovulation for the female rabbit, allowing her to be ripe for conception. The difference between this basic instinct among less evolved animals and humans is that it doesn't matter how attractive the female dog is to her male partner, or how long they have been courting or whether she has had her hair and nails done. It just matters that she's in heat. There is no pillow talk, no foreplay, just basic sex.

Human beings, on the other hand, learn to suppress their natural, basic sexual drive. We've learned that it's not socially acceptable to see couples having sex in public (unless you're at a swingers club!) just because the need or desire has arisen. We have lots of other rules around sex too—unlike primitive animals, for example, we are taught that it is against the law to have sex with a minor. We learn that we need to control ourselves and our primitive urges until the time and place are appropriate, even if this means that we may have lost desire by then. The other thing we have learned is that sex is a prized commodity, and we stereotypically believe that men need or desire it more than women. Therefore, we often use sex as a reward for good behaviour and pull back or withhold sex when we feel that our partner is undeserving. Sex, then, often becomes the prize, the dangling carrot! If he (or she) wants it, he has to behave himself—both in and out of bed. If he doesn't, we may even sacrifice our own desires in order to punish him. Over time, we get so good at this that we stop recognizing our desire to be touched, to be pleased, and to be sexual. In the end, we are punishing not only our partners but ourselves as well.

Over the course of my professional career, and even within personal circles, I have long known how rampant infidelity is. During the writing of this book, I have begun to realize, even more, how powerful a threat infidelity is to monogamous relationships. I recognize the importance of open, explicit communication and transparency as a way of combating the infiltration of those who have less respect for monogamous relationships. I realize that as human beings we are in need of emotional and physical connections with others, and that when either kind of connection is missing or neglected in a significant relationship, the fragile bond is even more vulnerable to being broken by others. But the broken bonds of monogamy cannot always be blamed on others. In monogamous relationships, we too are constantly fighting against personal temptation. When we realize that there are factors—like a lack of intimacy within the marriage—that increase the likelihood that you or your partner will give in to your urges or be less inclined to suppress your biological wants, we need to look at the real reasons that cause us to avoid sex and/or intimacy, and work physically and emotionally towards changing them. Many of us want what a monogamous relationship, in its ideal form, provides—to be able to share the joy of raising children together (if you choose) and to be able to grow together to the point that each knows what the other may be thinking, to share history that creates an unspoken bond, to be with a partner who has known your parents before they passed, seen you through your ups and downs, is there for you when you need a shoulder to cry on or to provide other emotional support. If you believe that this is worth fighting for, you need to work hard—to explore every possible angle of what has caused sexual intimacy in your marriage to deteriorate or vanish—and ultimately to create a stronger bond.

I'm also now more knowledgeable about ways to spice up a relationship and the importance of high sexual communal strength as a way of increasing the likelihood of creating and maintaining desire and a satisfying sexual relationship. I've learned that there is really no excuse for being bored in bed. This book, along with other resources in the form of books, workshops, and websites, are available to guide and assist you—you'll find many of these resources listed at the end of this book. If you want to explore alternate sexual lifestyles, you're living in the right century. Most societies are open to any and all forms of sexual exploration so long as it is between two or more consenting adults. No longer are sex and topics related to it taboo. With the Internet allowing us to access anything we desire, we can learn a lot of what we want to know more about.

In a slightly altered form, the title of this book poses a question: Why don't married people have sex? In a nutshell, I believe it's because they are not willing, or able, to discuss the truth about what is turning them away from their partners. As they say, the truth will set you free. If you've read this far, you should now have a much better understanding than you once did of the real reason (or reasons) that you're not into your partner, or not in the mood to have sex. Talk to him or her about it! Suggest that he or she read this book too. Figure out ways to work together at pushing the boulders out of your path, so that you can move towards enjoying one another and reconnecting on a deeply intimate and emotional level.

And what about the second question that the title asks (or suggests): Why are so many married men and women willing to engage in relationships with others, with or without the consent of their partners? I believe that it is not only because they are looking for something that is missing. For some, that something may never have been present. For many, what has gone missing has been gradual and normal—the desire to please, surprise, connect, and have fun with one's partner. For others, there's hostility, anger, disappointment, frustration, and resentment that lead to wanting to connect with someone who offers an escape. For others still, the cherry on top of an already sexually satisfying relationship can be hard to resist.

For some, the absence of sex is a deal breaker. Others continue to live with each another and do nothing about it, sometimes resenting the lack of intimacy and other times feeling grateful to have a caring partner, even if they are having very little sex.

My hope is that after reading this book, you will work your hardest to let your partner know what you are feeling and about your desire to connect with him or her before perhaps reaching out and connecting with someone else instead. When all is said and done, though, you need to ask yourself this question: How important an ingredient is sex in your relationship, and is your sex life an accurate barometer of your overall satisfaction as a couple?

The choice is yours. You are in the driver's seat. You can either continue on the same road or walk down the path towards inviting passion, eroticism, excitement, and pleasure back into your life with your partner—or someone else, after knowing the risks.

So, what will it be?

Acknowledgments

WRITING AND HAVING one's book published is never a solitary endeavour. Sure, the research and months of writing are typically done alone, but when it comes time to edit, print, bind, and market the book, part of its success is very much dependent on one's team.

Why Married Couples Don't Have Sex (. . . At Least Not with Each Other!) is my second book published by Simon & Schuster Canada. My first relationship book (following two parenting books) was published by Simon & Schuster in 2012. I knew then, as I know now, how fortunate I am to have such an amazing group of people rallying alongside me to the finish line and beyond. At the helm, publisher Kevin Hanson is one of the most humble, genuine people I know. Then associate publisher Alison Clarke was equally wonderful; she was approachable, available, and helpful—what more could I ask for? I also look forward to working with their incredible publicity, sales, and marketing team now that this book is released. I have no doubt that they will continue to support and work in partnership with me, as they did after my last book was released.

This is also the second time that I have had the pleasure of working with the editor S&S assigned to me—Linda Pruessen. Linda worked with me and J.M. (the co-author of my previously published book) a few years ago, and she was every bit as wonderful and easy to work with then. By the time that editing was complete, I had the feeling that Linda was as equally well versed on the content of this book as me and was every bit as invested in its success as I was. Working with Linda was fluid and easy. We share the same organizational skills and way of thinking and one of my fondest memories of working with her is sitting at my kitchen table—she with the entire manuscript printed out and marked up and I with my laptop open. Together, we spent hours going through the manuscript—page by page—with Linda offering me suggestions for improvement while I took notes on my computer so that I could tackle her requests later. There were many more back-and-forth email exchanges and revisions after that day, but each time, Linda's suggestions made sense, enabling me to produce the cohesive and well-organized book you've just read. Thank you, Linda, for the respectful, sensitive way in which you approached me when suggesting changes, for your warmth, partnership, and dedication to this project—Simon & Schuster sure has a knack for picking good people!

And speaking of good people, my deep appreciation and thanks go out to the many people, for the most part experts in their fields, who responded to my request for interviews and information so as to share their insights, anecdotes, and wisdom with me and you. Also, thanks to the clients who gave permission for their stories to be shared so that others might benefit from their experiences. The majority of case studies, however, are created from a compilation of stories that numerous clients have shared with me. None of their real names have been revealed and much of their stories have been changed so as not to identify their true identities.

I can, however, reveal the true identity of my wonderful agent, Chris Bucci, of Anne McDermid & Associates. Thank you, Chris, for your devotion, loyalty, and interest in my book ideas and projects ever since meeting you.

Aside from the wonderful people who helped bring this book to life, my husband and children have stood by my side, encouraged me, and believed in me always. This book is dedicated to my husband, Joey, for his unwavering support over more than thirty years. Not only has he encouraged me to pursue my dreams and shown such pride in my accomplishments, but he supports me by cooking and serving better meals than any restaurant I have tried! He's also a great listener and is always available to me and our children, no matter the time of night and day. Our children are growing and grown up. Talia graduated from university as a talented graphic designer and is working at an amazing agency in Toronto. There are not many things as rewarding as knowing that your child has found her niche and her passion—especially since I know what that feels like myself. Our younger daughter, Chloe, is in her second year of high school and is proving to be a hardworking student with a great deal of drive and ambition. She constantly amazes us with her wisdom and strength of character. Both Talia and Chloe have seen the fruits of labouring hard and, I'm proud to say, are following in our footsteps. Thank you, Joey, Talia, and Chloe, for your unconditional love and support.

And to other family members and friends, colleagues and clients who have long known about my passion for writing and my never-ending desire to share what I know in order to help others: thanks also to all of you for showing interest and support by listening and asking questions during and after the writing and release of this book.

Although I will likely take a break from writing to catch up on other projects outside of my counselling practice and to focus on my family before the kids leave the nest, I'm sure this book will not be my last. Until next time . . .

Notes

‿

How This Book Came to Be

1. E. Laumann et al., "Sexual Problems Among Women and Men Ages 40–80," *International Journal of Impotence Research* 17 (2005): 39–57.

Introduction: The State of the Union

1. The Kinsey Institute at Indiana University works towards advancing sexual health and knowledge worldwide. For more than sixty years, the institute has been a trusted source for investigating and informing the world about critical issues in sex, gender, and reproduction. For more information, visit www.kinseyinstitute.org.
2. Matty Silver, "How Much Sex Is Normal?" *Sydney Morning Herald*, February 4, 2014, http://www.smh.com.au/lifestyle/life/family -relationships-and-sex/how-much-sex-is-normal-20140204-31y41 .html.
3. Harry Fisch, "How Often Should You Be Having Sex?" *The Dr. Oz Show*, February 9, 2009, http://www.doctoroz.com/blog/expert -wxyz/expert-blog-wxyz2.
4. Tara Parker-Pope, "When Sex Leaves the Marriage," *New York Times*, June 3, 2009, http://well.blogs.nytimes.com/2009/06/03/when -sex-leaves-the-marriage/?_php=true&_type=blogs&_r=0.
5. "Sexless Statistics," Dr. Phil, http://drphil.com/articles/article/372.
6. Brian Clement and Anna Maria Clement, *7 Keys to Lifelong Sexual Vitality: The Hippocrates Institute Guide to Sex, Health and Happiness* (Novato, CA: New World Library, 2012), 12.

One: Sex Isn't the Issue

1. Alison Flood, "Fifty Shades of Grey Trilogy Has Sold 100m Copies Worldwide," *The Guardian*, February 27, 2014, http://www.theguardian.com/books/2014/feb/27/fifty-shades-of-grey-book-100m-sales.

2. One enterprising publisher and author (Marisa Bennett) even decided to seize the day and release *Fifty Shades of Pleasure: A Bedside Companion* (New York: Skyhorse Publishing, 2012).

Two: Is It All in Our Heads?

1. "The Dark Side of the Big 'O,'" Sexual Health Site, April 1, 2013, http://www.sexualhealthsite.info/the-dark-side-of-the-big-o-orgasms-sexual-arousal-limbic-system-dopamine-prolactin-oxytocin-coolidge-effect-sexual-infidelity.php.

2. "Your Brain on Sex," Reuniting: Healing with Sexual Relationships, June 26, 2005, http://www.reuniting.info/science/sex_in_the_brain.

3. Ibid.

4. See Betty Dodson with Carlin Ross: Better Orgasms. Better World, http://www.dodsonandross.com/about-us.

5. "What Are Some of the Funniest Sex Laws?" ChaCha, http://www.chacha.com/gallery/3094/what-are-some-of-the-funniest-sex-laws/28076.

6. Brian Clement and Anna Maria Clement, *7 Keys to Lifelong Sexual Vitality: The Hippocrates Institute Guide to Sex, Health and Happiness* (Novato, CA: New World Library, 2012), 25.

7. Edward O. Laumann, Anthony Paik, and Raymond C. Rosen, "Sexual Dysfunction in the United States: Prevalence and Predictors" *Journal of the American Medical Association* 281 (February 1999): 537–44, http://jama.jamanetwork.com/article.aspx?articleid=188762.

8. Harvey B. Simon, "Biking and Sex: Avoid the Vicious Cycle," *Harvard Health Publications*, September 14, 2012, http://www.health.harvard.edu/blog/biking-and-sex-avoid-the-vicious-cycle-201209145290.

Three: Excuses, Excuses

1. Accessed at http://www.reddit.com/user/throwwwwaway29 and http://newyork.cbslocal.com/2014/07/22/upset-husband-creates-spreadsheet-documenting-reasons-wife-has-refused-to-have-sex/.
2. "The Top Ten Excuses People Use to Avoid Sex," Rediff Get Ahead, September 17, 2009, http://getahead.rediff.com/report/2009/sep/17/top-10-excuses-people-use-to-avoid-sex.htm.
3. Devan McGuiness, "20 Excuses Women and Men Use to Get Out of Sex," Babble, http://www.babble.com/relationships/20-excuses-women-and-men-use-to-get-out-of-sex/.
4. Anke Hambach, Stefan Evers, Oliver Summ, Ingo W. Husstedt, and Achim Frese, "The Impact of Sexual Activity on Idiopathic Headaches: An Observational Study," *Cephalalgia* 33 (April 2013): 384–89, http://cep.sagepub.com/content/33/6/384.

Five: The Roommate Syndrome

1. "Sleep Study Reveals that 30–40 Percent of Couples Sleep Apart," *Huffington Post*, July 8, 2013, http://www.huffingtonpost.com/2013/08/07/sleep-study_n_3721615.html.

Six: All Stressed Out

1. Cheryl Fraser, "Your Questions on Sex, Love and Relationships Answered," *Best Health*, March/April 2014.

Eight: Left Cold

1. Betty Dodson with Carlin Ross: Better Orgasms. Better World. http://dodsonandross.com/about-us.
2. In the movie *Sex Tape*—released in 2014 and staring Jason Segel and Cameron Diaz as a couple struggling to spice up their sex life—the main characters use this self-help classic to inspire them to try out different positions as they create a sex tape of themselves.

Nine: Going Elsewhere

1. See http://www.truthaboutdeception.com/cheating-and-infidelity/stats-about-infidelity.html.
2. David Barash and Judith Lipton, *The Myth of Monogamy: Fidelity and Infidelity in Animals and People* (New York: W. H. Freeman and Company, 2001), http://www.worldcat.org/wcpa/servlet/DCARead?standardNo=0716740044&standardNoType=1&excerpt=tru.
3. Quoted in Brian Clement and Anna Maria Clement, *7 Keys to Lifelong Sexual Vitality: The Hippocrates Institute Guide to Sex, Health and Happiness* (Novato, CA: New World Library, 2012), 52–53.
4. "Do men really cheat on their spouses more than women do, or do they just get caught more often?" "Expert Center," *Prevention*, http://www.prevention.com/expert-center/do-men-cheat-more-women.
5. Robert Weiss, "Love and Sex in the Digital Age," *Psychology Today*, October 15, 2013, http://www.psychologytoday.com/blog/love-and-sex-in-the-digital-age/201310/women-who-cheat-relationships.
6. Ibid.
7. Clement and Clement, *7 Keys to Lifelong Sexual Vitality*, 45.
8. Russell B. Clayton, Alexander Nagurney, and Jessica R. Smith, "Cheating, Breakup, and Divorce: Is Facebook Use to Blame?" *Cyberpsychology, Behavior, and Social Networking* 16 (October 2013): 717–20, doi: 10.1089/cyber.2012.0424 717.
9. Russell B. Clayton, "The Third Wheel: The Impact of Twitter Use on Relationship Infidelity and Divorce," *Cyberpsychology, Behavior, and Social Networking* 17 (July 2014): 425–30, doi:10.1089/cyber.2013.0570.""
10. "Infidelity Statistics," Infidelity Facts, http://www.infidelityfacts.com/infidelity-statistics.html.

Eleven: Re-establishing Intimacy

1. Brian Clement and Anna Maria Clement, *7 Keys to Lifelong Sexual Vitality: The Hippocrates Institute Guide to Sex, Health and Happiness* (Novato, CA: New World Library, 2012), 133.

2. Taken from a poster at the 2014 Sexapalooza show in Toronto.
3. Julia A. Savacool, "Boring Bedroom Syndrome—It's Everywhere," WebMD, http://www.webmdcom/sex-relationships/features/boring-bedroom-syndrome-everywhere.
4. Clement and Clement, 7 *Keys to Lifelong Sexual Vitality,* 73.
5. Ibid., 66.
6. Ibid., 72.
7. Ibid., 73.
8. Stacey Grenrock Woods, "Thank You, Doctors: The Average Sex Time Is Not as Long as You'd Think," *Esquire,* June 30, 2009, http://www.esquire.com/women/sex/average-sex-time-0709.

Thirteen: When Things Don't Improve

1. Brian Clement and Anna Maria Clement, 7 *Keys to Lifelong Sexual Vitality: The Hippocrates Institute Guide to Sex, Health and Happiness* (Novato, CA: New World Library, 2012).
2. "It's True: Frequent Sex Is Healthy Sex," WebMD, November 22, 2012, http://www.webmd.com/sex-relationships/features/sex-use-it-or-lose-it.
3. Tara Parker-Pope, "When Sex Leaves the Marriage," *New York Times,* June 3, 2009, http://well.blogs.nytimes.com/2009/06/03/when-sex-leaves-the-marriage/?_php=true&_type=blogs&_r=0.

Resources

Books

Amen, Daniel. *Change Your Brain, Change Your Life: The Breakthrough Program for Conquering Anxiety, Depression, Obsessiveness, Anger, and Impulsiveness.* New York: Harmony, 1999.

Barash, David P., and Lipton, Judith Eve. *The Myth of Monogamy: Fidelity and Infidelity in Animals and People.* New York: Henry Holt, 2002.

Carnes, Patrick. *Don't Call It Love: Recovery from Sex Addiction.* New York: Bantam, 1992.

Clement, Brian, and Clement, Anna Maria. *7 Keys to Lifelong Sexual Vitality: The Hippocrates Institute Guide to Sex, Health and Happiness.* Novato, CA: New World Library, 2012.

Comfort, Alex. *The Joy of Sex.* New York: Crown, 2009.

Dodson, Betty. *Sex for One: The Joy of Selfloving.* New York: Harmony, 1996.

Fraser, Samantha. *Not Your Mother's Playground: A Realistic Guide to Honest, Happy, and Healthy Open Relationships.* Amazon Digital Services, Kindle ebook, 2013.

Gray, John. *Men Are from Mars and Women Are from Venus: The Classic Guide to Understanding the Opposite Sex.* New York: HarperPerennial, 2004.

Herz, Rachel. *The Scent of Desire: Discovering Our Enigmatic Sense of Smell.* New York: HarperPerennial, 2008.

Hirsch, Alan. *Scentsational Sex: The Secret to Using Aroma for Arousal.* London: Element Books, 1988.

Morgenstern, Michael. *How to Make Love to a Woman.* New York: Gramercy, 1989.

Neuman, M. Gary: *The Truth about Cheating: Why Men Stray and What You Can Do to Prevent It.* New York: Wiley, 2008.

Penney, Alexandra. *How to Make Love to a Man.* New York: Dell, 1982.

Ross, Carlin. *How to Make a Girl Come.* Smashwords, 2013.

Consumer Shows

Everything to Do with Sex Show (www.everythingtodowithsex.com)
The largest consumer adult and romance expo in North America. Features exhibitors, seminars, stage shows, celebrities, erotic art, kink, and everything in between. (In Montreal, Salon de l'Amouret de la Séduction: www.amouretseduction.com).

Sexapalooza (www.sexapalooza.ca)
A consumer show that offers a safe yet titillating environment dedicated to entertaining and educating on all aspects of sex and sexuality. Features stage shows, seminars, and shopping.

Taboo (www.tabooshow.com)
The Taboo Naughty but Nice Sex Show aims to encourage romance, personal betterment, and all things taboo. Features entertainment,

educational seminars, unique shopping, fashion shows, and live demonstrations.

Interviews

Anne Amitay, former owner, Lovecraft (www.lovecraftsexshop.com).

Dr. Laurie Betito, psychologist/sex therapist, host of "Passion," CJAD 800, president, Sexual Health Network of Quebec (www.drlaurie.com).

Noel Biderman, founder and CEO, Ashley Madison (www.AshleyMadison.com).

Dr. Rebecca Bodok, family physician and founder of Vital Transitions Clinic (www.vitaltransitions.ca/wordpress2/).

Carol Bresgi, founder and managing director, Canadian Men's Clinic (www.mensclinic.com).

Harvey Brooker, founder, Harvey Brooker Weight Loss for Men (www.harveybrooker.com).

Russell Clayton, doctoral student, University of Missouri (www.Russellbclayton.com).

Dr. Cheryl Fraser, psychologist (www.becomepassion.com).

Samantha Fraser, author, founder of Playground conference, "a sex positive inclusive event for all communities" (www.playgroundconf.com).

Daniel Gluck, founder, Museum of Sex, New York (www.museumofsex.com).

Carlyle Jansen, owner, Good for Her (www.goodforher.com).

Mercedes Jones, host of TV show, *Bringing Sexy Back* and owner, Dick and Jane Romance Boutique (www.dickandjane.ca).

Dr. Martin Jugenburg, plastic and reconstructive surgeon, Toronto Cosmetic Surgery Institute (www.torontocosmeticsurgery.com/).

Dr. Amy Muise, postdoctoral fellow, Department of Psychology, University of Toronto (www.amymuise.com).

Fiona Roche, social worker/psychotherapist and certified sex addiction therapist (found at International Institute of Trauma and Addiction Professionals, www.iitap.com).

Mikey Singer, vice president and show manager, Everything to Do with Sex Show (www.everythingtodowithsex.com).

John Sorensen, owner, Couples Resort (Algonquin Park, Ontario) (http://www.couplesresort.ca/).

Liz Lewis Woosey, president and show manager of Black Kat Shows (producer of Sexapalooza) (www.sexapalooza.ca).

Matt Poirier, owner, Club 4M (Menage à Quatre) (www.clubm4.com).

More Websites

2life (www.2life.io)

What began in 2004 as *2couples*—a print magazine—has since evolved into a digital magazine with lots of great information and advice. In 2013, they introduced a "communication" app not just for couples but for any two people who share a special or important relationship.

Betty Dodson with Carlin Ross (www.dodsonandross.com)
Betty Dodson and Carlin Ross are a team of intergenerational, sex-positive feminists whose dialogue on sexuality and feminism entertains and educates while delving into the politics of women's sexuality.

Everyone Loves Sex. So Why Wait?
(http://bryanasands.wordpress.com)
Pastor Bryan Sands's blog on sexual faithfulness.

Fetlife (www.fetlife.com)
A free social networking site run by kinksters for other kinksters (or those who are curious).

The Kinsey Institute (www.kinseyinstitute.org)
For more than sixty years, the Kinsey Institute has been a trusted source for investigating and informing the world about critical issues in sex, gender, and reproduction.

Museum of Sex, New York (http://www.museumofsex.com/)
Exhibitions, publications, and programs that bring the best of current scholarship on sex and sexuality to the widest possible audiences.

Not Your Mother's Playground (notyourmothersplayground.com)
A blog and ebook exploring the truth about open relationships.